Notes on
Conspiracy Theories

For much of my life I have been interested in the exploration, research and study of the assassination of President John F. Kennedy, since I first heard of the shooting while attending a high school typewriting class in Oklahoma in November 1963. Reading and thinking about the assassination is a hobby of mine. Some might call it a little more than just a hobby.

It's been a long, interesting journey of discovery. Over the years I've encountered theories that blame the murder on organized crime, the CIA, the Russians, American big business, aliens flying around in UFOs, and various influential politicians of that day.

But, no matter what conspiracy theory you examine, every single one that that I've looked at over the past fifty years has one name in common, one name that seems to always pop up somewhere in the course of the story. That name is H.L. Hunt, the oil billionaire.

John Curington's book, H.L. Hunt: Motive and Opportunity, *not only fans the flames of conspiracy theories pertaining to President Kennedy but also those involving Martin Luther King, Robert Kennedy and Jimmy Hoffa. In the rarified experience of reading this book, I could see a connection between these four killings and what Mr. Hunt may have had to gain from the death of these four men – probably more so than anyone else on the face of the Earth, in fact.*

This is Mr. Curington's story from his perspective as Mr. Hunt's right-hand man for many years, and he seems to suggest that if H.L. Hunt were involved in these deaths it was simply Mr. Hunt influencing other people who acted on their own to do these dirty deeds. In some ways that makes sense, because Mr. Hunt was spending millions of dollars on his daily Life Line *radio program, which was written and aired to influence listeners to accept his particular point of view.*

After reading an advance copy of H.L. Hunt: Motive and Opportunity, *however, I am more convinced than ever that Mr. Hunt did in fact have motive and opportunity in these deaths and was potentially more involved than anyone could possibly realize, including my friend John Curington.*

It is my firm belief that the accounts given in this book outline undeniable involvement, no matter what perspective Mr. Curington puts on them. For me, it is impossible to consider the fact that H.L. Hunt was not part of a potential conspiracy to "remove" these men, and I believe the book gives convincing evidence. I leave it to the reader to connect the dots in these four murders and draw his own conclusions.

– Dixon Cartwright

Powerful and popular men, each with a loyal, dedicated mind-made-up following, are the subjects of this book. Please read it with an open mind.

John Livingston

Mitchel White

H.L. Hunt:
Motive and Opportunity

by John Curington
as told to Mitchel Whitington

with a foreword by
Cyril Wecht, M.D., J.D.

ISBN 978-1-9393062-4-1

First Edition

Printed in the United States of America
Published by 23 House Publishing
SAN 299-8084
www.23house.com

Table of Contents

Introduction by the Author, Mitchel Whitington

In early May 2017 my telephone rang, and when I answered it I found myself talking to a man who introduced himself as John Curington – a name I'd never heard before. The man said, "I've been told that you are an author."

I confirmed that I was, and the gentleman said, "Well, I'm looking for someone to help me tell my story."

At that point, I was already mentally dismissing him. It was a request that I got from people all the time: "help me write my book." Most folks think that they have a wonderful story that the world badly needs to hear, but in reality, they probably don't. I politely told him that it really wasn't the kind of thing that I did – that I wrote my own books and generally didn't work with anyone else.

As I was looking for an opportunity to quickly end the call, he said, "I was H.L. Hunt's right-hand man for many years, and I believe that he could have had an influence on the deaths of John F. Kennedy, Martin Luther King, Robert Kennedy, and Jimmy Hoffa."

I stood there for a moment digesting what he'd said, and my next thought was, "Okay, this man has my full attention." We spoke for several more minutes and set up a face-to-face meeting for a few days later at a small eatery in Longview, Texas.

In the meantime, I did a little research and found out that he really was who he said he was, and that he might legitimately have a story to tell. I wasn't well-versed in

1

the story of H.L. Hunt, and although I knew about the four famous deaths that John had mentioned, I certainly wasn't that knowledgeable about them. I wondered what kind of stories this fellow had to tell about JFK, RFK, and the others... and since we would be talking about a presidential assassination – albeit one from half a century ago – I couldn't help but ponder whether the FBI would be tapping my phone if I started working with him on this project.

We met at the restaurant at the appointed time, and since it was mid-morning, the place was basically empty. John had already selected a corner table at the back of the dining room, his back against the wall, and when I sat down he began to talk. He'd brought a number of things to show me – books, papers, photocopies – and the more that he spoke, the more that I realized that he had some fascinating information, and I became more and more certain that I wanted to help him tell his story.

Probably the most interesting part of our first meeting happened when a clean-cut young man, perhaps in his mid-20s, walked over to our table and plugged his phone into an electric outlet right beside it to charge. With all of the other outlets in the empty restaurant, I thought that it was very strange that he selected one next to us. He then pulled a chair over to it as if to wait on his phone to charge, which basically put him at our table.

We'd been discussing the assassination of JFK in Dallas back in 1963, so for a fleeting moment I almost panicked, wondered just how many times we'd uttered the phrase "killing the president" without specifically mentioning JFK.

It was more than a little awkward with this stranger having invaded our space and our conversation. Things got even weirder, however, when his first comment to us was, "Are you guys talking about Trump?"

I thought, "Oh my Lord, this guy is FBI, CIA, or maybe NSA... what in the world have I gotten myself into?"

John and I wrapped things up, choosing to go outside to finish our conversation. I half expected for the young man to follow, but he didn't. As I drove away, I couldn't help but glance in my rearview mirror to see if anyone was tailing me. I wondered what this book experience was going to be like if odd things continued to happen.

As it turned out, nothing like that happened again. Looking back, I believe that the young man was just a random coincidence... but it did give me a pretty good story to tell.

After working with John to put his story into this book, I've got to admit that he has a very interesting tale.

Conspiracy theorists may be a little disappointed in John's stories, since they don't put H.L. Hunt on the grassy knoll as JFK's motorcade went by in 1963; outside the Lorraine Motel in Memphis, Tennessee in April of 1968; at the Ambassador Hotel in Los Angeles in June of 1968; or even outside the Machus Red Fox Restaurant in suburban Detroit in 1975. No, there aren't any smoking guns tying Mr. Hunt to the murders of JFK, MLK, RFK, or Hoffa.

Instead, John Curington has a collection of true stories – vignettes of his experiences with Mr. Hunt – that he wants to record for posterity. Some of them raise a number of questions, so it would be easy to turn these into

3

sensational, speculative stories, such as why Mr. Hunt met with Marina Oswald, or why he sent $40,000 to a man in Los Angeles after RFK's assassination, but instead, John simply wants to tell what happened from his perspective.

There's a lot of nobility in that. I can't tell you how many times I've sat across the table from him and heard him say, "I don't want to try to convince anybody of anything; I just want to tell my story."

And for that reason, it's been a genuine pleasure and honor to be part of this project. And with that, I'll leave you to Mr. John Curington to tell his own story. I hope that you enjoy it as much as I have.

– Mitchel Whitington

Foreword by
Dr. Cyril Wecht, M.D, J.D.

As a forensic pathologist, I have spent many years of my life studying the assassination of President John Fitzgerald Kennedy; I was the first civilian who was ever given permission to examine the Kennedy evidence and autopsy. I've written over twenty books, a number of them on the Kennedy assassination, and I routinely speak at conferences around the country on the subject. The killings of President Kennedy, of his brother Bobby, and Dr. Martin Luther King have been more than a casual interest in my life.

In each case, research reveals many more questions than answers. In the case of John F. Kennedy, the strange circumstances start almost with the moment of his death. When that pronouncement was made, the body should have legally been turned over to Dr. Earl Rose, the Dallas County medical examiner, who was present at the time. Dr. Rose was a forensic pathologist who was well-respected in the medical community. Secret Service agents were loading the body into a waiting ambulance, and when Dr. Rose tried to intervene, he was slammed up against the wall by the Feds, hands on guns, and threatened with profanity-laden language. They took the body of the president illegally out of the city in violation of the laws of the city and county, and those of the state of Texas.

5

Instead of assembling a team of the country's top forensic pathologists to examine the body, three military officers were selected to perform the most important autopsy in our nation's history. While they were all fine men and probably good doctors, two of them were not forensic pathologists, and neither of them had ever performed a single autopsy involving gunshot wounds. The third officer was a forensic pathologist, but he had never functioned in that capacity in any coroner's office. Not a single person in the autopsy room had the education, the training, or the experience to handle the task that faced them.

That was apparent in their findings. Initially, they even missed the fact that the president had a gunshot wound to the throat. The autopsy was a comedy of errors, but that information was presented to the Warren Commission as the facts of the case.

The president was shot on Friday, November 22, 1963, at 12:30 pm. By Monday morning, FBI Director J. Edgar Hoover was already announcing that Oswald had acted alone. By that time, of course, Oswald had already – conveniently – been killed. No in-depth investigation had taken place, but Hoover was proclaiming the facts about what had happened less than seventy-two hours after the assassination. That alone should have raised the collective eyebrows of the nation.

There are issues with the Bobby Kennedy case that are just as interesting. Probably the least known, but most damning item comes from the autopsy, which was one of the finest that I have ever reviewed. It was thorough and by the book, the complete opposite of the one performed on JFK.

The autopsy, however, showed that Robert Kennedy was killed by a shot fired from only an inch to an inch-and-a-half behind his right ear, even though witnesses indicated that Sirhan Sirhan fired from a few feet away at the front of the senator. There is unanimity of opinion concerning the rear head-shot among all the forensic pathologists who were present at the autopsy, including military personnel... yet this fact was never introduced into the trial.

Also, there were thirteen shots fired that evening... although Sirhan was holding an eight-shot Iver Johnson .22 caliber Cadet 55-A revolver. Three shots hit Senator Kennedy, two lodging in his body and the other passing through his arm. Five other bullets hit five other victims without exiting their bodies. The LAPD found three other bullet holes in the foam ceiling and two more in the door-frame to the pantry in the kitchen of the Ambassador Hotel where the shooting occurred. Officers removed the wooden door-frame and burned it – another case of material evidence being not only mishandled but deliberately destroyed.

The case of James Earl Ray, accused assassin of Martin Luther King, is just as strange. He was a two-bit, punk thief – a penniless bum who was in jail for most of his adult life. Ray was not political, not an activist, and seems to have had no overwhelming motive for murdering King.

In fact, after he allegedly shot Dr. King, James Earl Ray was kind enough to leave a Remington 30-06 rifle – complete with his fingerprints on it – for the authorities to discover. I have to assume that he wanted to give the police a head start on finding him. He fled the country and was with not one, but two fake passports; this petty criminal was traveling with false credentials that would make would make James Bond green with envy.

As a forensic pathologist, much of my focus has been on the events that took place after each of the killings. Of course, there has always been a huge question about the series of events leading up to the killing of the president. There have been many theories, but unfortunately, most everyone from that time is gone – for years we have relied on second-hand accounts to piece the events together.

Some time ago I received a phone call from a man who identified himself as John Curington, the right-hand man to H.L. Hunt for many years. He told me that he had a story to tell that possibly involved Mr. Hunt in the murders of John Kennedy, Martin Luther King, Robert Kennedy, and Jimmy Hoffa.

Of course, I was immediately intrigued, and after expressing my interest, we hung up the phone and John Curington overnighted me a rough draft of the book that he had written on the subject. Once I picked it up, I could not put it down. I read the book in short order, and then called him back the next morning to discuss it further.

This book was interesting for many reasons, not the least of which is that he does not put forward any particular conspiracy theories, as many books on the subject do. Instead, he merely tells his own story and allows the reader to extrapolate what might have happened.

This is an incredibly important story because as John said to me, he is the last man standing from that era. Imagine talking to a man who could pick up the phone and call J. Edgar Hoover or Lyndon Johnson – John could, and often did. He is the man who arranged for $40,000 to be delivered to a Los Angeles hotel after Robert Kennedy was killed, who delivered $125,000 in a briefcase to James Earl Ray's attorney after Martin Luther King was assassinated, and who met with an associate of Jimmy Hoffa before his release from prison.

Most interesting to me, he saw H.L. Hunt meeting with Marina Oswald, he helped organize an anti-Kennedy campaign on Hunt's *Life Line* program, and he personally heard H.L. personally utter the prophetic words, "I've about got a bellyful of those Kennedy boys. They both need to go."

I have spoken with John on a number of occasions and personally met with him for several hours in Dallas one enjoyable afternoon. I can tell you that John Curington is the real thing, and his story may impact the history of these events as we know it today.

I believe John's story is that important, which is why I sent him the letter that follows.

– Dr. Cyril Wecht, M.D, J.D.

27 March 2018

Dear Mr. Curington,

Your close personal relationship in the 1960's with H. L. Hunt, then often referred to as the richest and most influential man in the world, gave you a front-row seat on events surrounding the deaths of John F. Kennedy, Martin Luther King, Bobby Kennedy, and Jimmy Hoffa.

My professional medicolegal and forensic scientific background, plus more than 50 years of study, research, and investigations, also provides me a front-row seat on these same events.

Letter from Dr. Wecht to John Curington

The world deserves a more thorough, objective and honest closure of these deaths.

With a joint venture between the two of us, we can arrive at some critical suggestions as to how to achieve such closure.

Best wishes on this endeavor, your first book. Hopefully, my brief comments will be of interest to your readers.

Kind regards,

Sincerely,

Cyril H. Wecht

P.S.: Do you think we could get a federal grand jury to open the JFK assassination?

Letter from Dr. Wecht to John Curington (page 2)

Part I: My Name is John Curington

In the late 1950s and early 60s, H.L. Hunt always had a booth for his *Life Line* radio show at the State Fair of Texas. Mr. Hunt used that program to spread his own message against things that he didn't like, among which were the Kennedy brothers, Martin Luther King, and labor unions, to name a few.

The booth was large, with several chairs, free drinks and a complete display of *Life Line* literature. The booth was staffed by attractive young ladies who handed out *Life Line* material and answered questions about the program.

We reached a lot of people with the booth, so Mr. Hunt came up with the idea of expanding the program's exposure by getting *Life Line* space at the New York 1964 World's Fair, which would begin on April 4 that year.

Although this would be an avenue for great publicity, it would also cost a lot of money. On the other hand, investing in the World's Fair could bring in a good bit of income as well. To offset the cost, Mr. Hunt elected to make the effort to rent World's Fair space that would both generate revenue and provide an outlet for advertising *Life Line*. Mr. Hunt and I traveled to New York and met with Robert Moses, the man in charge of the fair.

Early at our first meeting, Mr. Moses leaned over to Mr. Hunt and said, "Do you know why I am in charge of the New York 1964 World's Fair?"

Mr. Hunt simply replied, "No."

13

Moses said, "It's because I am the meanest, toughest son-of-a-bitch in New York, and everything goes my way."

I didn't have to be around Robert Moses very long before I began to believe that he was one of the most arrogant, self-entitled, pompous men that I'd ever met.

Nevertheless, a deal was struck whereby we would obtain exclusive rights to operate a complete amusement park and food center. I don't recall the amount of money that Mr. Hunt paid for that right, but it was a substantial amount.

The New York World's Fair (photograph by Ron White)

The next step was to buy and install all of the midway rides. I had made contact with a New York man who sold German-made rides to other amusement parks across the United States.

I needed to leave for Germany immediately, but I didn't have a passport. At Mr. Hunt's suggestion, I called Vice President Lyndon Johnson to see if he could help us out, and he was able to get a government employee to come to our room at the Waldorf-Astoria and take care of everything from the application to the photograph. Someway, somehow I was issued a new passport within forty-eight hours – hand delivered to my hotel room.

I flew to Germany and Mr. Hunt spent about $1,300,000 for some of the premier rides in the world, including a carousel with hand-carved animals, and the ever-popular Wild Mouse roller coaster, one of the most popular rides of the day. In today's world that monetary figure would equate to over ten million dollars.

A Typical Wild Mouse Roller Coaster Ride

I paid for the rides with a check and arranged for all of them to be shipped to New York. On the way back home, I went to Switzerland and picked up $1.5 million dollars cash for Mr. Hunt; but that's a story for later in this book.

Meanwhile, we began hiring men who had experience in amusement rides. At that point, it looked like the entertainment park of the World's Fair was going to be a roaring success.

Everything was going great; we had purchased popular rides, we had them in New York, and a skeleton crew had been formed to assemble and install them. Mr. Hunt had purchased a three-bedroom house close to the fairground that would not only be our living quarters but would satisfy all of our office needs as well.

In the middle of October 1963, Robert Moses requested that both H.L. Hunt and I come to his office immediately. When we arrived, Moses very succinctly stated that he believed Mr. Hunt only wanted to be a part of the New York World's fair to expose his *Life Line* agenda to the public. Moses then went on to say that a *Life Line* political message was not welcome or wanted there

Robert Moses

and that he was, therefore, canceling the agreement on the spot.

I'll never forget how he did it. Moses looked right at Mr. Hunt, and without even blinking said, "You know, black people don't like you... Jewish people don't like you... poor people don't like you... the president doesn't like you... and I don't like you."

I could immediately tell that Mr. Hunt was not only angry at the contract suddenly being canceled but was even more outraged at the way that Moses had done it. No one spoke to him like that – ever.

It wasn't just an emotional issue, though. By that time we had an incredible amount of both time and money invested in the project, and it looked like a lot of it was going to be lost.

After simmering over the whole thing for a bit, Mr. Hunt finally called Vice President Lyndon Johnson for advice and perhaps some assistance with the matter. LBJ's response was that he was already aware of what had happened, but the decision to take H.L. Hunt out of the New York World's Fair was made by a "higher authority," and that his hands were tied in the matter.

Lyndon Johnson

Under the terms of the terms of the original agreement that Mr. Hunt had signed, Robert Moses actually did have the authority to cancel the contract with or without cause. While he had to right to do so, the way that he did it infuriated Mr. Hunt.

We ended up with over a million dollars of hard-to-sell amusement rides, a $75,000 New York house that we didn't need, a $15,000 car for us to use while in the city, and thousands and thousands of dollars spent on hirings and other incidentals... not to mention a year-and-a-half's time investment, which was almost impossible to put a dollar figure on.

Finally, we were able to sell the rides themselves for about twenty cents on the dollar. In an even worse twist of fate, the buyer filed for bankruptcy before we even received the first payment. No money was ever collected – it was a complete and total loss. All in all, Mr. Hunt lost well in excess of two million dollars cash on the venture, which was a huge sum of money in those days... over sixteen million dollars today.

H.L. Hunt believed that the "higher authority" LBJ had spoken of when he'd called him was none other than President Kennedy himself. Mr. Hunt felt that the United States president had him kicked out of the New York World's Fair for no other reason than the fact that his *Life Line* program had been broadcasting a strong anti-Kennedy message for some time.

When we were on an airplane back to Dallas, Mr. Hunt looked over at me and said something that I'll always remember. "John," he told me, "I've about got a bellyful of those Kennedy boys." After a pause, he added, "They both need to go."

Well, not long after we were kicked out of the World's Fair, Mr. Hunt came to me and said that he needed to send $70,000 to someone in Chicago. There was a man there whose name was Ed Bodine who we knew from that city, and he was to be the one that delivered the money. Mr. Hunt trusted him, which was important

18

because that was a lot of money – it was the equivalent of over half a million dollars in today's world.

Ed owned a plant in Chicago that we did a lot of business with, so Mr. Hunt knew that he would be happy to take the money back and make the drop... without charging anything for doing so.

I called Ed on Mr. Hunt's behalf, explained the situation, and asked him to fly to Dallas to pick up the cash. When he arrived I was waiting for him at the airport, and I drove him to Mr. Hunt's office. We visited for a few minutes, and then Hunt wrote out a check to himself for $70,000 and gave it to me to cash.

I took an elevator down – the Hunt offices were in the Mercantile Bank Building – and I went to the large-transaction teller window. The bank was very accustomed to me handling deposits and withdrawals of that size.

I was given a bank envelope that had seventy one-thousand dollar bills, and I went back upstairs and gave it to Mr. Hunt. I told him that I was taking Ed to lunch, and we'd be back for the money after that.

Later on, we got back to the office and Mr. Hunt wasn't there. The envelope was on his desk, however, so I picked it up and gave it to Ed, and then took him to the airport and dropped him off for his return trip to Chicago.

By the time I got back to the office, I was told that Ed had already tried to call me a number of times, and he wanted me to sit there and wait for his next call. When he finally reached me, he was in a full-blown panic mode. The first words out of his mouth were, "I just counted the money, and there is $5,000 missing!" Ed went on say that there was no way in the world that he could deliver a package that was less than what the receiver was expecting. He knew, as I did, that if the amount was short he would not be allowed to leave the drop... unless it was in a body bag. Money hand-offs could be that serious.

I knew Ed well enough that I certainly didn't suspect him of taking the money, and I definitely didn't take it, so that only left one person: Mr. Hunt. I'd seen the world's richest man short-change people before in gambling deals and such, so this wasn't all that unusual. Five thousand dollars would be such a small amount of money to him that it clearly wasn't about the cash – it was all about control and power. He knew that I wouldn't say anything about it to him, and Ed wouldn't either. I doubt he gave any thought at all to the consequences of the delivery being made $5,000 short. As I've said before, he didn't think like you and I do.

The problem was that the missing amount could literally cost Ed his life once the person receiving the money realized that it was short. I had to do something to help him out.

Since I didn't have an extra $5,000 in my wallet, I drove to my bank and took out a loan for that amount. When I got the cash I went straight to the airport, gave Ed the money to bring the amount back up to the $70,000 that he was expected to deliver.

As grateful as Ed was, he told me that he didn't have that much money back home to repay me – understandable, because five grand back then is the equivalent of around $40,000 today. He told me that he had a number of items that he would be sending me that would more than make up the money, though.

Sure enough, I received a number of things from Ed over time that paid me back for the loan I had taken out. I don't know where or how he got them; I just know that he was good to his word.

I know that this is a fantastic story, bordering on the unbelievable. Imagine going to work tomorrow and learning that your boss had taken $40,000 out of the till, and since you couldn't confront him about it, you had to go to your bank and take out a personal loan for that much money to make it up... without any absolute guarantee that you'd be reimbursed, of course. Well, this did really happen, and for me, it was just another day at the office.

There are some subtle things about the story that you might have missed, however. The first is that when Mr. Hunt removed the money from the original bundle, he did so without any consideration for the consequences that might befall anyone else. If Ed hadn't counted the money, he could have easily delivered an amount that was short back in Chicago, and depending on who the receiver was, could have lost his life for doing so. It would never have occurred to Mr. Hunt to think of anyone else, though.

The next curious thing was the mysterious identity of the person in Chicago who received the money. Mr. Hunt had apparently told Ed who that was, but I never knew. If I had to guess, I'd say it was a crime figure – after all, legitimate business deals were never transacted in cash. I'd heard a Chicago man named Sam mentioned by Joe Civello in his conversations with Mr. Hunt, and perhaps it was that person.

The other interesting thing concerns the $70,000 itself – the equivalent of over half a million dollars in today's money. I'd hand-carried many gambling debt payoffs for Mr. Hunt, yet he didn't want me delivering this money, or knowing who it was going to. Instead, he wanted Ed

Bodine from Chicago to carry this money to whoever the recipient was. The timing is very curious – this was just a short time after the World's Fair fiasco and a few months before John. F. Kennedy was assassinated.

After that, with LBJ in the Oval Office, both Bobby Kennedy and Martin Luther King could be kept in check. Even though Mr. Hunt continued to criticize them with his *Life Line* program, and worried about their influence on the country, the two men went about their business. When Lyndon Johnson made the decision not to run in 1968, however, both of those men were killed within two months of each other.

One more thing – I mentioned that I got my passport in a highly unusual manner, and I used it for many years. When it expired, I got another and finally a third. No matter where I traveled, or how often, a stamp was never placed in my passport by any foreign country. They would look at it and just wave me through.

To this day I have been puzzled about this – I don't have an explanation or answer. I sometimes wonder if my first passport – since it was arranged for me by LBJ himself – had some code that allowed me to simply pass through. When I went to Germany to purchase the rides, for example, everyone was being pulled over to the side in customs for further examination, but I was simply waved right through... with no entry stamp from the country. I guess I'll never know the truth about the passport that I was issued by LBJ's people.

An Opening Statement

My name is John Curington; maybe you've heard of me, maybe you haven't. I've certainly been the subject of a good bit of speculation over the years. Some folks that I've never actually talked to have written things that I supposedly told them directly and others have woven me into stories in my role with H.L. Hunt. While some of them are certainly true, some definitely aren't. I just felt like it was time for me to set the record straight.

As an attorney, I always get to make an opening statement when starting a case in court. While this isn't a courtroom, I would like to take a moment and do just that.

After I'd had a couple of meetings with Mitchel Whitington, we made an agreement to work together on my book *H.L. Hunt: Motive and Opportunity*. One of the things that I asked for was the chance to make an opening statement that he would include as written... so here it is.

Haroldson Lafayette Hunt is the center of my story, but the other famous men involved are: John Fitzgerald Kennedy, killed on November 22, 1963; Martin Luther King, killed on April 4, 1968; Robert Francis Kennedy, killed on June 6, 1968; and Jimmy Hoffa, who disappeared (and was presumably killed) on July 30, 1975.

I have the utmost respect for Mr. Hunt. He provided jobs for thousands of employees; he produced and distributed products such as oil, gas, food, and more which filled the needs of people not only in our country but around the world as well.

Mr. Hunt viewed himself as a down-to-earth, honest man, and in many respects, he was. On the other hand, he was the richest man in the world, and so there was nothing out of his reach.

People with that kind of money simply don't think like you and I do. He could buy anything that he wanted,

23

but wore suits off the rack and carried his lunch to work in a brown paper bag. He could pick up the phone and call some of the most powerful men in the world with the ease that you or I would phone our next-door neighbor. The only rules that he played by were the ones that he made, and for the most part, he wasn't answerable to anyone in the world.

For example, as the richest man in the world, the U.S. Internal Revenue Service kept a close eye on Mr. Hunt and his dealings. To my knowledge, he never cheated on his taxes, but he used every available legal avenue to avoid paying what he didn't have to. More than that, however, since the IRS had an agent assigned strictly to him, Mr. Hunt set up an office for that agent in our building. I personally made sure that it was a large office with a magnificent view of downtown Dallas.

That's me –
John Curington

It had a radio, television, private telephone, and every other amenity that I could think of. Mr. Hunt never had a problem with the IRS.

I'm going to tell you my story in order. First, a bit about myself so that we can get a little better acquainted. Next, some background on Mr. Hunt – if you don't understand him, the rest of the book won't make as much sense. In fact, I have some individual stories and vignettes from my time with Mr. Hunt that will help paint a picture in your mind. I particularly like the taxi story and the pocketknife story, because they really help show who he was... but we'll get to those in short order.

Finally, there are four different sections about the men I mentioned earlier: John Kennedy, Martin Luther King, Bobby Kennedy, and Jimmy Hoffa. I want to tell you not only about Mr. Hunt's dealings with them, but the motive and opportunity that he had to influence the circumstances surrounding their deaths.

Before we get started, I'd like to sincerely thank you for taking the time to listen to the account of my time with H.L. Hunt. I think that everyone from casual readers to historians to hard-core conspiracy theorists will find it interesting.

Now, An Introduction

I was born in Collin County, Texas, in a city named Farmersville. I had a very common, uneventful boyhood life. My father and mother were hardworking farm owners and enjoyed a good reputation in the agricultural community.

Back then Farmersville was called the "Onion Capital of North Texas" and shipped over a thousand carloads of onions every year – that's train boxcar loads, by the way. The place was very serious about its onions.

During the time that I worked on the family farm, there were also four brothers named Murphy who worked with me from time to time: Audie, Buck, Dick, and James.

Audie would go on to become the most decorated World War II hero and a successful movie star. As an adult he became good friends with H.L. Hunt – through

25

that relationship, I was able to help Audie on some of his personal projects.

Farmersville, Texas in 1900 – Many Years before My Birth

During the mid-1940s, it was common for high school boys to hitchhike from Farmersville to Dallas on any given Sunday. Don't ask me why; it was just something we did. Once we got to Dallas, we'd simply turn around and hitchhike back home.

I know that it sounds like a waste of time, but to us, it was a glorious adventure. Whether the thrill was a trip to "Big D," or simply getting forty-something miles out of our little town, we looked forward to it on the weekends. In those days, hitchhiking was a safe venture – that was a much simpler, more innocent time.

On one particular Sunday morning, Audie's brother, Dick and I decided to make the Dallas run. And then something very strange happened.

Our first lift took us as far as McKinney, and we were waiting to catch another ride on to Dallas. A car stopped, and the driver said that he was going that far and would be happy to take us along. Before he got to town, though, he was going to stop at his airport and fly his airplane. He asked if we'd like to go for a flight.

For two boys who'd never been in an airplane before, this offer was a dream come true – we both jumped at the opportunity.

The plane was a single-engine open cockpit, and you had to be strapped down to the seat. We each were given a pair of goggles along with a leather cap for our heads, and the man took off. As soon as we were airborne, he took us straight up in the air vertically and straight back down again. He flew in tight circles banking first left and then right, and it wasn't long until both of us boys were airsick.

To be honest, I didn't know whether we were going to live or die. Neither one of us had given any serious thought to what could actually happen on our first airplane ride.

He finally – mercifully – landed, but Dick and I were both too sick to get out of the cockpit. The pilot lifted each of us out and propped us up against a tree in the shade. Seeing that we were still too shaken up to travel, he left us there unattended and continued on to Dallas. We sat under that shade tree for a few hours without food or water and finally recovered to the point that we could walk.

We went back to the highway and hitched a ride back to Farmersville. Personally, I didn't get on another

27

airplane until the U.S. Army flew me from Los Angeles to Korea.

The entire event was strange and surreal, but the reason that I wanted to share this particular story is that it is such a perfect metaphor for the rest of my life.

In the same way that I have no idea how or why I happened to be picked up that day by a pilot who wanted to take me for a wild airplane ride, I have no idea how or why that a few years later I was selected to take another kind of wild ride – working directly for a man named H.L. Hunt.

After high school, I continued to work on the farm, which was not a bad deal at all. Because I had a Texas driver's license at the age of twelve, I got to drive tractors, cars, and trucks. Time passed, and I rode horses and swam in the river when I wasn't working. It was a wonderful time for a young man.

I eventually went off to Baylor University in Waco and was then drafted into the Army. After basic training and being commissioned as an officer, I was stationed in South Korea until my discharge, at which time I went to Dallas and had my first job interview.

In 1954, at the age of thirty-two, I started working for Hunt Oil in the land division. The country was divided into separate areas; my job was to review all of the oil and gas leases for the eastern part of the U.S. and present them to Bunker and Herbert Hunt (H.L. Hunt's sons) for directions on whether to keep or release each one.

I'd been working there for only a few years when the lady on the switchboard called and told me that H.L. Hunt wanted to see me. That kind of thing simply didn't happen to employees at my level, so I was sure that someone was playing a prank on me. I remember thinking that if it wasn't a joke and Mr. Hunt really did want to see me, it couldn't be good. In that case, it was probably time to pack up the things on my desk and polish up my résumé.

I said as much to the telephone operator, who assured me that it was not a trick, nor was it a mistake. I heard a click on the phone, and the next thing I knew, I was talking directly to Mr. Hunt.

He simply said, "My sons Bunker and Herbert tell me that you're a man who knows how to get things done. I want you to come to my office." I did so, met with Mr. Hunt, and after a short conversation, I was directed to take the office adjoining his.

I was H.L. Hunt's right-hand man for a number of years... his personal assistant, his go-to guy whenever and for whatever he needed to be done. I wasn't his adviser or confidant, and we didn't have long, personal conversations; he had no interest in my counsel or advice. Whenever he needed something done, he let me know, and I did it without question or hesitation. I was very successful in that role.

My office adjoined his, and the door between them was never closed. I could see everyone who came to meet with him and heard most every conversation; he didn't care if I heard his, nor did I care if he heard mine. Very little went on in Mr. Hunt's office that I didn't know about.

There was a button on Mr. Hunt's desk that he could push that sounded a buzzer in my office; this was a signal that he wanted me to come in. We also had a code with the buzzer when I was to get someone out of his office.

I had been working for Mr. Hunt only a short time when he called me in and said, "John" – he always just called me John – "I have a gold mine in Colorado, and I either want to sell it or shut it down. Go check it out for me."

Having received my instructions, I went back to my office and thought about it for a few minutes. I finally got my courage up and went back to talk to Mr. Hunt. I said, "I believe that you've picked the wrong man for this job – I don't know a thing about mining or gold."

Without missing a beat, he said, "That is exactly why I chose you. If you knew anything about it, you would be gone three or four days, and then return with a report that said nothing; you would not get the job done. Because you don't know anything about it, you'll be able to simply give me the facts." He went on to say, "My ideas of a business assignment are very simple. I only want to know what it takes to get in, what it takes to get out, and what will be left over afterward."

During my first few days of working directly for Mr. Hunt, I was trying to finish a big land deal that I had been working on. Mr. Hunt told me to turn it over to someone else; he said, "Keep this in mind – deals will be around a lot longer than the money. Tomorrow you will probably have a deal that is bigger and better than whatever this one is."

Another off-the-cuff assignment came my way one morning. Mr. Hunt called me in and said that he and his son Lamar had agreed to move Lamar's old football team, The Dallas Texans, out of Dallas. I was told to find a new city to relocate them.

Of course, I knew that this was a big assignment because Lamar would probably expect me to devote a lot of time and money towards making a decision for the new location.

Dallas Texans Logo (from the author's collection)

I went into my office and looked at a map of the United States that was on my wall and had an idea. I began sticking pins into every city that had a professional football team. It soon became obvious that Kansas City was wide-open country – another football team wasn't even close.

I then took out a book that had a listing for all of the radio and television stations within 150 miles of Kansas City, and I saw that there were a good number of them. Seeing that, I had my answer. I walked back into Mr. Hunt's office and said, "Kansas City is the best place in the U.S. for a football team."

If I do say so myself, in today's world, any large research firm would take many months and probably charge six figures to come up with such an important recommendation as to where to move a football team. By simply using a little common sense, though, it's something that I managed to do in just two hours. I was mighty proud of that.

As an aside, there was a signed contract between Lamar Hunt and Clint Murchison regarding the move of the football team. Clint owned the Dallas Cowboys, Lamar owned the Dallas Texans, and there were some anti-trust laws to contend with. You just couldn't pay off someone not to compete with you. Both men knew that Dallas couldn't support both teams, and one of the two had to move. There is a rumor that the decision was made with the flip of a coin. In any case, both parties agreed in writing that one would move and the other would stay. After this had been done, Lamar Hunt and Clint Murchison also agreed to destroy the contract upon completing the terms – after all, it was proof of a violation of the anti-trust laws. I retained a signed contract for my file, which I still have to this day.

Working for H.L. Hunt, I didn't question his orders, and I didn't try to analyze the things that he did or didn't do. I simply followed his instructions to the best of my ability and tried to survive.

Mr. Hunt did have a lot of quirks, however. I remember one time during the holiday season when a long-time employee, an accountant, came into my office. He handled both legal accounts for the company and all of Mr. Hunt's personal business. All in all, he'd been an employee for over twenty years, but he had never worked directly for the big boss. He stood at my desk and told me that he'd received a Christmas card from Mr. Hunt, and he wanted him to sign it as a keepsake. As we were talking, I heard Mr. Hunt's voice call out from his office. "Who's in there?"

I called back with the gentleman's name.

"Who's that?" was the reply.

I said, "He's your personal accountant."

Mr. Hunt then said, "Well, what does he want?"

"He'd like you to autograph his Christmas card."

"We didn't send *him* one, did we?" Mr. Hunt said in a rather disgusted voice. The accountant turned around and left. That odd little exchange was fairly typical of how surreal many of my experiences at Hunt Oil were.

I was more or less on long-term call; Mr. Hunt would contact me anytime something crossed his mind. I remember one night I was in bed sound asleep when my telephone rang. I picked it up and heard Mr. Hunt's voice ask, without any salutation or greeting, "How many times is aloe vera mentioned in the Bible?" I knew that he had been looking into the health benefits of that particular plant, and I assumed that this request had something to do with his curiosity about it. I told him that I didn't know, but I would find out. The next morning, I called Southern Methodist University's Perkins College of Theology and posed the question to someone I knew there, and I was able to report the exact number of Biblical references back to Mr. Hunt later that day. In case you were wondering, aloe vera is mentioned in the Bible six times.

Most of Mr. Hunt's requests weren't that whimsical. To my personal knowledge, H.L. Hunt sent two different employees to Switzerland to pick up a large sum of cash. The first to make this trip was H.L. Williford in the mid-1950s, and after his trip, he kept a letter in his file that he had taken to present to the bank; I still have that letter.

I was the second Hunt employee to do this. My trip was in 1963; I was already in Germany to buy amusement rides for Mr. Hunt's contract with the 1964 New York World's Fair. From there I was to go to Switzerland, and I had a very similar letter with me, the body of which read:

Swiss Bank Corporation
Zurich, Switzerland

    Please pay to the bearer of this letter the sum of one million five hundred thousand and no/100 dollars ($1,500,000.00) and charge to my account No. 79329 in your bank. Please accept this letter as your receipt for these funds.
    Sincerely,
    H.L. Hunt

My assignment was to pick up $1,500,000.00 in cash. When I went into the Swiss bank, I was met at the door by the president. I presented the letter; he took me to his office, and after pleasantries and a short visit, he said, "I have your money ready for you – do you want to count it?" He opened a briefcase that was filled with money.

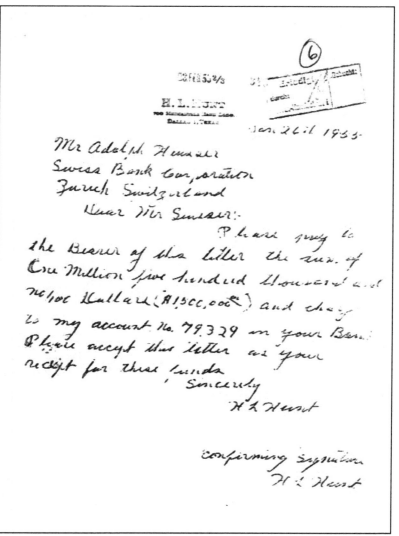

The Zurich Bank Letter

I told him that counting it was not part of my instructions, so the bank president closed the briefcase and handed it to me. There was no checking of identification, no signing of papers, no receipts, nothing like that at all – I just took the briefcase to the airport, and then back to the U.S. where I handed it directly to my boss, H.L. Hunt. He didn't open it in front of me, and I never saw the briefcase again.

This may seem strange in today's post-9/11 world, but in that day and age there was no airport security to dig through your bags, or x-ray your carry-on. You just walked out to the plane and took your seat. I do have to admit, though, that it felt a little strange flying across the ocean with one-and-a-half million dollars in a case at my feet.

Because of my position with H.L. Hunt, I entered into a fairy tale environment that I never knew existed prior to that. Every door I entered in the course of my job was already open for H.L. Hunt. I just slipped in on his coattail.

To this day, I do not know why H.L. Hunt called me when I worked in the land office. I had never met him, talked to him, or had any exposure to him whatsoever. My résumé would certainly have not attracted anyone's attention.

For the next several years, my exposure to the fairy tale continued. I met extremely important people throughout the United States and even the World. Those people never knew me by anything other than, "That's the Hunt man."

And Mr. Hunt always took care of me – I'm not trying to brag, but he apparently valued my services so much that on July 17, 1965, he gave me a letter that gave me an incredible amount of security. It said the following:

Dear John:

In consideration of and payment for certain personal services and duties that you have performed for me individually, for the Hunt Oil Company and for other Hunt entities, I have agreed, and this letter reduces to writing my agreement, that you are to have lifetime employment with the Hunt Oil Company, its successors or assigns, said employment to be for as long as you live or for as long as you desire.

Your salary will be maintained at a level with others of equal abilities employed by the Hunt Oil Company and your salary will never be reduced from the high point that you have reached.

I have further agreed that as additional consideration for your personal services and duties that in the event Hunt Oil Company or its successors or assigns or any other Hunt entity elects to terminate your employment at any time and regardless of the cause or reasons for such termination, then Hunt Oil Company, its successors or assigns, will pay to you the cash sum consideration of Two Hundred Thousand dollars, said payment to be made immediately at the end of your termination of employment.

This letter is a binding obligation on Hunt Oil Company, its successors or assigns, and a binding obligation on me individually and my heirs and assigns.

With best wishes...
Constructively,
H.L. Hunt

H. L. HUNT
1401 ELM STREET
DALLAS, TEXAS 75202
July 17, 1965

Mr. John Curington
2119 Province Lane
Dallas 28, Texas

Dear John:

    In consideration of and payment for certain personal services and duties that you have performed for me individually, for the Hunt Oil Company and for other Hunt entities, I have agreed, and this letter reduces to writing my agreement, that you are to have life-time employment with the Hunt Oil Company, its successors or assigns, said employment to be for as long as you live or for as long as you desire.

    Your salary will be maintained at a level with others of equal abilities employed by the Hunt Oil Company and your salary will never be reduced from any high point that you have reached.

    I have further agreed that as additional consideration for your personal services and duties that in the event Hunt Oil Company or its successors or assigns or any other Hunt entity elects to terminate your employment at any time and regardless of the cause or reasons for such termination, then Hunt Oil Company, its successors or assigns, will pay to you the cash sum consideration of Two Hundred Thousand dollars, said payment to be made immediately at the end of your termination of employment.

    This letter is a binding obligation on Hunt Oil Company, its successors or assigns, and a binding obligation on me individually and my heirs and assigns.

    With best wishes...

This Agreement Is
Accepted By Me:

John Curington

Constructively,

H. L. Hunt

H. L. Hunt
Individually and as President of Hunt Oil Co.

The July 17, 1965, Letter

38

There is another letter that Mr. Hunt gave me and two of my associates that I kept as well. It is on Mr. Hunt's personal stationery, and is dated September 7, 1966. With that letter, Mr. Hunt allowed me the latitude to enter business deals on my own while working for him. Later on, people would accuse me of wrongdoing in that regard, but as you can see, I did so with Mr. Hunt's blessing.

September 7, 1966

To whom it may concern:

This letter is to confirm that I have given consent and approval to John Curington, Paul Rothermel and B.M. Rankin, Jr. to enter into some transactions for oil and gas deals and other business activities for their private account while employed by Hunt Oil Company.

In giving this consent, each has agreed to treat this matter highly confidential and not to divulge to others, and especially Hunt employees, any information or details concerning this arrangement.

Each one concerned is signing this letter to acknowledge a pledge to conduct all these operations confidential in a businesslike manner and in accordance with our agreement.

> *<signed>*
> *John Curington,*
> *Paul Rothermel,*
> *B.M. Rankin, Jr.*
> *H.L. Hunt*

H. L. HUNT
1401 ELM STREET
DALLAS, TEXAS 75202
September 7, 1966

TO WHOM IT MAY CONCERN:

This letter is to confirm that I have given consent and approval to John Curington, Paul Rothermel and B. M. Rankin, Jr. to enter into some transactions for oil and gas deals and other business activities for their private account while employed by Hunt Oil Company.

In giving this consent, each have agreed to treat this matter highly confidential and not to divulge to others, and especially Hunt employees, any information or details concerning this arrangement.

Each one concerned is signing this letter to acknowledge a pledge to conduct all these operations confidential in a business-like manner and in accordance with our agreement.

John Curington

Paul Rothermel

B. M. Rankin, Jr.

H. L. Hunt

The September 7, 1966, Letter

This book is relayed in the deepest respect for H.L. Hunt. Still, I know of no other person in the world who has had such a close exposure to John F. Kennedy, Martin Luther King, Bobby Kennedy, and Jimmy Hoffa.

Each of the four men did have – or could have had – a great deal of negative influence on many of H.L. Hunt's business activities. Each one of them was assassinated. Although Hoffa's body was never discovered, it's a fairly safe bet that he was murdered on the day that he disappeared.

In this book, I'll pose the questions that I have often asked myself about the death of these four men...

Did Mr. Hunt have a motive?
Did Mr. Hunt have the opportunity?
Did Mr. Hunt have any influence?
Did Mr. Hunt fit into a conspiracy?

For anyone who reads this book, it is my desire that each reader will review the different stories and reach a conclusion not on my story, but on what common sense would suggest the answer to be. Again... was there motive, opportunity, influence and conspiracy? It's your decision.

Finally, let me say that there have been any number of things written about me in books, articles, online, etc. – some good and some bad. It's not my intention to try to defend one story or deny another. I don't want to argue with anyone about anything or try to persuade someone to believe one thing or another.

My name is John Curington, and I simply want to tell my story.

41

Part II: H.L. Hunt

To fully understand my story, you first have to take a look at the man whose given name was Haroldson Lafayette Hunt. Of course, I always just called him, "Mr. Hunt," and to this day I still do.

In 1948, the media referred to H.L. Hunt as "the richest man in the world." At the time his assets were estimated at $263 million, which would be the equivalent of $2.6 billion in 2017 dollars. Most people can't fathom the term "richest man in the world" and what it *really* means. To the average person, it simply implies that he can drive the best car and doesn't have to worry about how much a loaf of bread costs at the grocery store.

To fully appreciate the extent of H.L. Hunt's wealth, however, you have to understand that as an individual citizen – a single person – he was one of the world's largest private landowners; private cattle owners; private oil and gas producers; food producers; petroleum refinery producers; private employers; and farm product producers.

At the time of his death in 1974, his fortune was estimated at approximately $5 billion – which would be $25 billion in 2017 dollars.

As a person, he was a very complex man. He presented himself very differently to individuals; everyone who met him had a completely unique opinion and experience.

That doesn't surprise me – in fact, it was something that Mr. Hunt prided himself on. Back in the day, I saw one of his kids go into his office to talk to him about some issue, and they would discuss it for a while and he or she would leave completely satisfied. A while later, another one of his kids would come in to discuss the same thing, and Mr. Hunt would give him or her a totally different story – and of course, he or she would leave completely satisfied. I would hear everything because the door between our offices was never closed, and I came to realize that he enjoyed playing with people in his own private little game.

I came to understand that Mr. Hunt did what he wanted, when he wanted, without concern for stepping on anyone's toes. When he decided on something, he went after it without thinking of anyone else.

All this came from a very humble beginning. H.L. Hunt was born on February 17, 1889, on the family farm near Ramsey, Illinois. He was the youngest of eight children and was educated at home.

As a teenager, he set off on his own and finally settled in Arkansas. By the age of twenty-three he was running a cotton plantation, and when the plantation was destroyed by flooding, he turned to his pastime of gambling to generate income. A big win in a card game enabled him to buy his first oil well in El Dorado, Arkansas. By 1925, he had amassed a small fortune of over half a million dollars, which he then began to deplete through over-drilling and bad investments.

H.L. Hunt in 1911

Rumors began to surface about a huge oil field in neighboring East Texas, so he turned his sight in that direction. All but broke, on November 26, 1930, he used $30,000 that was borrowed from a businessman in El Dorado to buy into a deal with Columbus M. "Dad" Joiner, the wildcatter who had discovered the East Texas field. Hunt reinvested his profits back into the business and that eventually made him the owner of the well and Joiner's other leases in the area.

East Texas Oil Field, 1919

By 1936, the East Texas Oil Field was a booming operation, and a headquarters for Hunt Oil was established in Tyler, Texas. A few years later, the business was moved to Dallas, and in 1938, H.L. Hunt paid $69,000 for ten acres of land on White Rock Lake. A version of George Washington's Mount Vernon stood on the property that was larger than the original and became the home of the H.L. Hunt family.

Hunt Oil Company became a behemoth in the world of petroleum – it was one of the largest producers in the country by the 1940s. During World War II, it sold the majority of the oil used by all of the Allies combined. More Hunt oil was sold to the U.S. and the Allies than the entire country of Germany produced on its own during the war.

As the war ended, Mr. Hunt was supplying natural gas to a good part of the United States. He then began to look beyond his oil and gas business and soon expanded into consumer goods through a company called HLH Products, which was about the time that I moved from the Land Division to Mr. Hunt's office.

I worked for Mr. Hunt for a relatively long period of time – you see, he had an extremely low tolerance for anyone who worked directly for him. With very few exceptions, most people who reported directly to him lasted only two or three months. I believe that I had such a long tenure because of three things:

1) I never spoke to him frivolously or made small talk. For example, I never said "Good morning," "Good evening," "Did you see the game last night," "See you tomorrow," or anything else like that.

2) I never asked Mr. Hunt a personal question on any topic – his home, family, health, car, leisure life, etc.

3) I never made any reference whatsoever to my own personal life. I didn't mention my activities outside the job, my family, or anything else that didn't directly involve my employment.

I'd figured those things out early on, and I think that explains my longevity with Mr. Hunt. These items definitely governed my interaction with him. Something that was just as important was that I never spoke about Mr. Hunt's business with anyone – not even my family. Because of that, he entrusted me with matters that very people knew about.

Not the least of these was his juggling of three different families, something that I was completely privy to, and helped him coordinate.

Mr. Hunt and Lyda

Mr. Hunt was still a young man who was seeking his fortune in Arkansas when he began dating seventeen-year-old Mattie Bunker, escorting her to social events around the city of Lake Village.

In1914, Mattie's sister Lyda came back home for a visit from Jonesboro, where she was a teacher. Lyda was twenty-three at the time.

Haroldson Lafayette Hunt was instantly and completely infatuated with Lyda – not only her brown eyes and dark hair but her cultured demeanor and intelligence. He was stricken and began courting the older sister. They were married that same year.

Lyda was with him through those early days, as he moved from the wells of Arkansas into the East Texas Oil Field, to Tyler, and finally to their Mount Vernon home in Dallas.

Together they had seven children: Margaret (born 1915), Haroldson ("Hassie") (born 1917), Caroline (born 1923), Lyda (born 1925), Nelson Bunker (born 1926), William Herbert (born 1929), and Lamar (born 1932). Lyda died as an infant at only one month old, and Hassie suffered a host of mental issues that basically incapacitated him in adulthood. The other five children were the ones that we always referred to as the "first family." H.L. and Lyda remained married until her death in 1955.

Mr. Hunt and Frania

When his daughter Lyda, his wife's namesake, died in infancy, Mr. Hunt was grief-stricken and fell into the arms of a woman named Frania Tye.

Frania was a real estate salesperson that he had met in Tampa, Florida. Mr. Hunt was in Florida to investigate a real estate boom there, but instead, he met Frania, introducing himself as Maj. Franklin Hunt.

As the story goes, the couple began a romantic relationship, and although he was still married to Lyda, H.L. Hunt is rumored to have married Frania in Ybor City, Florida on November 10, 1925.

After their alleged marriage, Mr. Hunt and Frania began a family of their own. Her four children by Hunt were: Howard (born 1926), Haroldina (born 1928), Helen (born 1930), and Hue (born 1934). Mr. Hunt is said to have spent his time bouncing back and forth between the first family in Arkansas and the second family in Florida.

To make matters a bit more convenient, Mr. Hunt finally moved the Frania family to Dallas, and the first family to Tyler, Texas.

More and more rumors were starting to circulate about H.L. and Frania, and when Lyda learned of the family – and H.L. Hunt promised that the relationship was over with Frania – Lyda offered to bring the four children into the family and adopt them. Frania would not hear of such a proposal, however.

At one point in the relationship, Mr. Hunt tried to get Frania to convert to Mormonism – not for any religious reasons, but instead because he felt that the Mormon faith would allow the bigamy that he was involved in with Lyda and Frania.

Frania eventually learned about the marriage to Lyda in 1934 after having allegedly lived with Hunt for nine years. She testified in court that they were in a room at the Adolphus Hotel in downtown Dallas when he suddenly

49

peeked out into the hallway, then locked the doors and made sure that their conversation was private. Mr. Hunt then offered her one million dollars to sign a document saying that they were never married. She exploded, screaming and yelling at the Texas billionaire.

Nevertheless, she finally did sign the document and received approximately a million dollars in the form of cash, trust funds for her four children, and a $2,000 monthly payment.

Mr. Hunt hired a man named Col. John Lee to marry Frania, which he did. For this, he received a monthly salary of $1,200... which in today's world would be the equivalent of about $20,000 every month. It was a great arrangement for Lee, because not only did he get an exorbitant salary, but he was given a beautiful home in a classy neighborhood, an automobile, and domestic help... all that and, as a bonus, Frania was an attractive woman. It was a good deal for him. Frania eventually divorced him, but not before she took his name for herself and for her kids.

When Mr. Hunt died and his will was read, Frania was shocked to learn that neither she nor her children were mentioned at all. She was irate and flew into a rage, and finally, she and her son Hue decided to file a lawsuit against Ray Hunt, Hunt Oil, and the H.L. Hunt estate in 1975. They wanted to have Frania declared as the putative wife of Mr. Hunt, her children recognized, and one-half of all Mr. Hunt's Louisiana assets.

According to a story in the *Indianapolis Star* on July 12, 1981, when Frania and her son Hue were preparing for the lawsuit, they were looking for an official record of the marriage. They found "a voided entry in a marriage-license receipt record book that showed the names 'Franklin Hunt' and 'Frania Tye' for the date Nov. 10, 1925. But no sooner had the attorneys in the case of Lee vs. Hunt made certified copies of the document than someone came along and sliced the original out of the record book with a sharp-edged instrument."

The newspaper article goes on to say, "Along with the disappearance of the marriage record came another startling development. According to Hue, nearly all of his mother's photographs and 16-mm film of H.L. in the old days was stolen from Frania's Atlanta home. As in the case of the marriage record, no culprit was apprehended."

The lawsuit was one in which both parties paraded all the family's dirty laundry through the court. I was called as a witness by Hue Lee and testified in the case.

The lawsuit was vicious, and both sides were angry, but it finally ended in a settlement. Although I've seen a number of different figures, as I recall the recognized Hunt heirs would pay $6 million. Half would be paid from the trusts of Lyda's children, the other from the trusts of the third family, which we'll be talking about shortly. The money would go to Frania, her children, and her grandchildren – but they agreed to drop any claim as legitimate heirs to H.L. Hunt.

I remember that even though Frania's son Hue had agreed to the deal, when it came down to signing the final papers, everyone did so but him. The trial had been so taxing on all parties involved that the judge reportedly signed Hue's name to it himself to simply end the whole ordeal.

Mr. Hunt and Ruth

While Mr. Hunt ended his relationship with Frania, he didn't settle down into monogamy. He soon started a new relationship with a woman named Ruth Eileen Ray, a "voluptuous secretary" who worked in his oil company. The *Washington Post*, in an article published on July 12, 1981, reported that Mr. Hunt had first seen her standing at a bus stop and offered her a ride. They quoted Mr. Hunt as saying, "We drove out into the country. The dogwood was in bloom."

Ruth gave Mr. Hunt four children: Ray (born 1943), June (born 1944), Helen (born 1949), and Swanee (born 1950). I always called them the "third family."

It is said that the oldest son, Ray, was responsible for the marriage of Mr. Hunt to his mother. As the story goes, two years after Lyda Hunt died, 14-year-old Ray showed up at the Hunt Oil office in Dallas, and told Mr. Hunt, "You will marry my mother."

According to the *Washington Post*, "Not long after, Hunt ate Sunday dinner with two of his daughters, and then excused himself, saying he had 'an appointment.' The first that the daughters or their brothers would know of the wedding was an announcement the next morning in the *Dallas Times-Herald*."

After their marriage, Mr. Hunt adopted Ruth's four children, and she later admitted that they had been his biological children all along.

Even though she and Mr. Hunt had been having an extra-marital affair that produced four children, it is said that Ruth was responsible for Mr. Hunt's conversion to Christianity – he and his kids were baptized by Dr. Criswell of the First Baptist Church in Dallas.

In reality, I believe that this was a contrived business move by Mr. Hunt. He did very little in life that wasn't carefully orchestrated to either protect or advance his business. Ruth introduced Mr. Hunt to the Reverend Criswell, and Mr. Hunt surely knew that he was one of the most powerful Protestant ministers in America. In my opinion, from all my years of working with Mr. Hunt, I think that his miraculous conversion was much more about business than spirituality.

The Three Families

I think that having three simultaneous families speaks volumes about H.L. Hunt. It confirms that in the quest to satisfy himself, he had no thoughts at all about the effect that it might have on others. The three different ladies who thought that he loved only them, the children that were born out of wedlock... all this was done to satisfy Mr. Hunt, even though the situation caused many problems for all of them – and for the surviving kids, even to this day.

In her book *H.L. and Lyda*, Hunt's daughter Margaret quoted her mother Lyda as saying, "Daddy always said that his genes were so outstanding that he wanted to leave a lot of them to the world. I am certain that he does not imagine there is anything the matter with this. He is so naïve."

I believe that being a child of Mr. Hunt's – in any of the three families – was both a blessing and a burden. All of his children went on to be extremely successful, and were very active in charitable endeavors... something that being a Hunt child afforded them. On the other hand, there had to be a lot of pain in knowing that your father had three separate families, each unknown to the others for some time.

Someone that I am acquainted with who worked with Helen Hunt, a daughter in the third family, told me that Helen actually kept two diaries. One was for her day-to-day life, while the other was used to record her feelings of anger, pain, and anguish concerning her father. I can certainly understand that.

Personally, I was privy to all three families from the start, just as I was to much of Mr. Hunt's business, both public and personal. Because of my position, I had to walk a tight-rope. I knew all three wives and all fourteen children and had to deal with them on Mr. Hunt's behalf. I would move money for them into the accounts that he specified, and help him coordinate his activities with them, both after they learned about each other, and before they knew the truth.

Hue was probably the most aggressive of all the kids and would come into the office from time to time. In the mid-1960s, he wanted to make a movie called *What Am I Bid?* starring Leroy Van Dyke, Tex Ritter, Faron Young, and more. Mr. Hunt gave him four hundred thousand dollars to make the movie, which he actually did get made in 1967. He apparently did a fair job, because in today's world the *Internet Movie Database* rates it as a 7.3 out of an overall score of 10.

There are many stories about Mr. Hunt's kids, especially as they got older, but my role was to simply do what Mr. Hunt needed to be done to manage the three families, without commenting on the situation or passing judgment.

Getting to Know Mr. Hunt

It may puzzle a lot of folks when they consider the fact that Mr. Hunt was juggling three families, fourteen kids, and three wives – although, granted, Frania was never legally able to establish their marriage.

This is all a very telling thing about Mr. Hunt. Not only did he believe that he could do or have anything that crossed his mind, I believe that he thought he was doing the world a favor by leaving behind a large number of children.

As a final family note, Mr. Hunt once confided in me that he really had married Frania Tye, and he also said that he was certain that one of his children by Lyda wasn't his, because the child would have had to be conceived at a time when he was with Frania. I said that on the stand during a trial in which I had been called to testify, so argue about it as people will, it is now a part of the legal record.

Before getting into the stories of Mr. Hunt and JFK, MLK, RFK, and Hoffa, I want you to get to know him. There are dozens of biographies that tell the basic facts about his life. They are rigid and sanitized, and although you would learn the elements about him, you still wouldn't really know Mr. Hunt.

No, I believe that the best way to get to understand Mr. Hunt is the way I did – through personal experiences with him. I could fill a book with interesting stories about the man, but I've selected a few to illustrate his life and his way of thinking.

Some are interesting, others entertaining, but I hope that overall they will provide a background for his thoughts and attitudes, and to why he felt that there was no problem in inserting himself into national events, maybe even the deaths of JFK, MLK, RFK, and Hoffa.

Accompany me, if you will, into the life of H.L. Hunt...

Mr. Hunt and the Movie Stars

H.L. Hunt was never one to be star-struck or enamored with Hollywood types, although he did brush shoulders with them occasionally.

He visited with John Wayne, Bing Crosby, Bob Hope, and some of the other biggest names in the industry. It could be that they knew that he was incredibly wealthy and simply wanted to make sure that he was aware of them in case he ever financed a film.

On his side of it, Mr. Hunt probably knew that they wielded incredible influence on the American people, and wanted to keep up a relationship with them in case they could ever be an advantage to him in business.

I remember that there was an exclusive "African Safari Group" with a number of movie star members, and William Holden once sent Mr. Hunt a complimentary membership card to the club – it was 24-karat gold.

On another occasion, when Mr. Hunt met Tex Ritter, the star of many westerns, he told him, "I notice that you always wear two six-guns on your belt... that makes me think that you're not a very good shot!"

I saw only one time when money or favors passed between Mr. Hunt and Hollywood. He called me one day and said, "I need $25,000 cash to give to Bob Hope. Take it out of the Reliance Trust." I did so without question, but I seemed to remember that the particular trust fund had been set up for Frania Tye and her kids, and typically a trust fund isn't touched by the person who sets it up. Nevertheless, I got the money together in cash and gave it to Mr. Hunt to pass to Bob Hope. I have no idea what the money was for, and I never heard anything else about it.

Although he did occasionally rub elbows with the stars, I can honestly say that I never knew Mr. Hunt to be a movie fan. He didn't go to see a lot of films, with one exception: James Bond, 007. Whenever a new Bond film was released he would go to the theater and see it – I think that all of the power and intrigue appealed to him.

Leisure and Entertainment

In all the years that I worked for Mr. Hunt, I never saw him devote a lot of time to leisure activities – other than gambling, that is.

While he had all the resources at his disposal for a wonderful lifestyle, I never saw him take advantage of them. For example:

- Hunt properties around the country had some of the best fishing rivers and lakes in the world, but he never went fishing.
- His land holdings had incredible natural game hunting, yet he never went hunting.
- Some of the Hunt investments were resort golf courses, but he never took up the game.
- He owned more cattle and horses than he could even count, but he never pulled on a pair of cowboy boots and never rode a horse.
- No matter how many times we went to New York, he never took in a Broadway play; and he never shopped on the exclusive Rodeo Drive on his trips to Los Angeles.

- He never had anyone stop by the office just as a friend; if someone did get in, it was strictly for business, and took place in a three to five minute period.

This list could go on and on, but it is probably obvious that everything that H.L. Hunt did was for H.L. Hunt and his business – except for gambling, which was his one avenue of entertainment, even though the rest of the entire world was completely open to him.

I do recognize and agree that almost everyone, including family members, would have stories that gave a completely different view of him from the points listed above. But Mr. Hunt had the talent and ability to conceal his own personal thoughts and beliefs and make those in his presence believe that they knew the real H.L. Hunt. He could project any image that would benefit him.

The New York Taxi Ride

Mr. Hunt and I were in New York and staying at a very nice hotel, the Waldorf-Astoria. We had an appointment early one morning with the president of the A&P Tea Company. We left the Waldorf-Astoria that morning at 7:30 am to be at the 8:00 meeting. The president's office was in a building just a short distance from our hotel.

That particular morning it was raining and the weather was terrible. We flagged down a cab, got in, and gave the driver directions. At the first street past the hotel, Mr. Hunt told the driver, "Turn here." The driver kept going another block before turning. Traffic was heavy, the rain was still coming down, and in two or three minutes we were at our destination. The meter on the cab showed a fare due of ninety-five cents.

A typical New York Taxicab

We got out of the cab, standing in the rain without umbrellas or raincoats, and Mr. Hunt gave the driver a one dollar bill and said, "Keep the change."

The driver was visibly upset and ranted that he was entitled to a larger tip. Mr. Hunt told him that if he had turned when he was told, the fare would have been about forty-five cents and he would still have received a dollar. His tip would have been fifty-five cents in that case. The driver did not accept this explanation and was still demanding a larger tip.

Mr. Hunt was upset, even though he was soaking wet. He then demanded that the driver give him his nickel change back. The driver refused, saying that when Mr.

Hunt told him to keep the change he lost the title to the nickel.

Finally realizing that it was a standoff, Mr. Hunt walked away, and I followed. We were both soaking wet – all over a five-cent tip. Remember, at this time, Mr. Hunt was still being referred to as the "world's richest man."

The Pocket Knife

H.L. Hunt's empire operated worldwide and involved thousands of employees. For the business to run smoothly, it required many key, qualified employees. When Mr. Hunt selected a leader, that leader was given complete authority to just "get the job done."

One morning Mr. Hunt called me and said that he had just lost his pocket knife and had to get a new one. He always carried one, so he wanted to get the replacement right away. There was a downtown sporting goods store just a few blocks away from our office called Cullen and Boren – I told Mr. Hunt that I would just get an employee to run over and pick him up a new knife.

He replied, "Hell, I'm not going to turn my knife-buying over to someone else!" That said, the two of us walked over to Cullen and Boren and spent a couple of hours there. I watched as Mr. Hunt inspected every knife, and finally selected one that cost about $20. At a $5,000,000 a day income I have no idea how much money was lost on this two-hour shopping trip, but at least Mr. Hunt got to pick out the pocket knife that he wanted.

I also found it very strange that he routinely trusted people to purchase millions of dollars of oil equipment, but wouldn't trust an employee to pick out a knife.

One of the main things that Mr. Hunt used his knife for was to crack pecans. He ate pecans year-round for a couple of reasons; the first of which was that he was convinced of their health benefits. The second was that he was the owner of the largest pecan grove on the North American Continent.

He would crack the pecans against the handle, and eventually broke off a piece of it.

Mr. Hunt's knife with the broken handle

This was a Case Double-XX knife, stamped "USA," which is highly collectible. It served him well over the years, but at one point someone that we did business with in the pecan industry sent Mr. Hunt a gold pecan cracker that fit in his pocket.

He liked it so much that I fell heir to the pocket knife, which I still have to this day. It's a nostalgic reminder of Mr. Hunt.

The Waldorf-Astoria

On our frequent trips to New York, Mr. Hunt and I always stayed at the Waldorf-Astoria Hotel. From time to time we would be on the same floor as General Douglas McArthur, who often stayed there as well.

When this happened, we would sometimes share a dinner with the general in Mr. Hunt's room, which was usually attended by other high-ranking military officers.

Mr. Hunt always wore a suit with a bow tie. Not only was a bow tie cheaper than a long tie, but it was also easier to put on. This, unfortunately, gave him the appearance of an elevator operator at the hotel.

He was actually mistaken for such a person on a particular afternoon at the Waldorf-Astoria. We had just stepped into the elevator, and although Mr. Hunt was standing at the front by the elevator panel, I reached out and pushed the button for our floor. As the door was closing, a middle-aged woman dashed in; she glanced at Mr. Hunt and curtly said, "Ninth floor."

Mr. Hunt just stood there. He didn't move, say a word, or in any way acknowledge the woman's presence as the elevator continued toward our destination.

Glaring at him, she repeated, "Ninth floor." The woman sounded a little put out at that point.

Again, there was no acknowledgment by Mr. Hunt, although it was clear to me that she had mistaken him for an elevator attendant. I was more than a little amused at that point, but I didn't say anything – I wanted to see what happened next.

The woman was becoming visibly angry. "I said, ninth floor! Are you deaf, or just a dumb-ass?" Glaring at Mr. Hunt, the richest man in the world, she snapped, "I will have you fired before the day is over!"

The elevator then stopped at our floor, the doors opened, and we stepped out. We left the lady unattended in her quest to find the ninth floor.

At this time in his life, Mr. Hunt had a number of different bank accounts that could easily cover the purchase price of the entire Waldorf-Astoria Hotel itself, yet because of his ordinary clothing, he'd been mistaken for an employee – an elevator operator. Although I was greatly entertained by the whole thing, I never said a word to Mr. Hunt… I'm not sure that he was at all amused.

KERA Channel 13 and the Hunt Documentary

In mid-1965, the Dallas TV station KERA Channel 13 was presenting a documentary program on H.L. Hunt. KERA had aired the Hunt program more than once, and we learned that it was set to be aired on several future occasions.

H.L. Hunt liked the program because it presented him in a very constructive light, so he wanted it to continue airing. Not only that, but he also wanted to do something that would get more viewers to tune into any future broadcasts.

At that time, the H.L. Hunt offices were in the downtown First National Bank Building, which was adjacent to and overlooked the KERA building. In the lobby of the First National Building, there were several pay telephones for the public to use. About 1:00 pm one particular day I went down to the lobby and used one of those phones to call KERA. When their receptionist answered, I said something to the effect of, "If you air the H.L. Hunt program one more time, someone is going to blow your entire building off the face of the Earth!" I hung up after that and quietly took the elevator back up to my office.

Of course, this was just a false threat on my part – I had no intent to cause any harm whatsoever. I never would. My plan was simply to get more exposure for the H.L. Hunt story and in turn get more viewers to watch the show.

My office was on the 25th floor at that time, and I happened to glance out of the window toward the KERA building. I saw a police car driving up with its lights flashing. It was closely followed by a number of fire trucks and other emergency vehicles. I quickly turned my office television on, changed the channel to 13, and saw that KERA had stopped all programming and was devoting their broadcasting strictly to the bomb threat. The police wanted to evacuate the surrounding buildings, the hoopla continued to grow, and soon all the Dallas radio and television stations were reporting the "bomb threat" event.

Mr. Hunt and I continued to watch the drama unfold. I have to reiterate that there was no harmful intent at all... but we did take pride in getting more coverage on the H.L. Hunt story. Because of all the publicity, KERA did continue to air it, although, in the future, we tried to avoid any further promotional ideas along that line.

```
                 B O M B     T H R E A T


         At noon today, Radio Station KERA Educational

    Television, according to the Criminal Investigation

    Detachment, received a telephone call from a raspy

    voiced elderly sounding man who said, "if you run that

    program on H. L. Hunt one more time I'll bomb your

    television station". The caller than hung up.



                           ###
```

Press Release issued by KERA

The Two H.L.s

Without a doubt, H.L. Williford was the closest and most trusted man who ever worked for Texas oil billionaire H.L. Hunt. He was a close friend and a very dedicated employee. Mr. Hunt's enormous wealth was the result of H.L. Williford helping Hunt acquire the East Texas Oil Field from the original drilled as the Daisy Bradford #3 well from Dad Joiner. At this time the three of us – Hunt, Williford, and myself – were living in New York at the Waldorf-Astoria Hotel.

I had been away in Germany, but upon my return, I walked into an explosive situation. The two H.L.s had been in a heated discussion over some kind of personal problem.

65

When he and Mr. Williford had acquired the East Texas Oil Field, Hunt had promised Williford lifetime employment.

For reasons unknown to me Mr. Hunt had fired Mr. Williford and ordered him out of the hotel and back to Dallas. This wasn't entirely surprising, because even though they were friends, disputes between the two H.L.s were common. This time seemed different, however, more intense. Mr. Hunt said in no uncertain terms that Mr. Williford was to never set foot onto any Hunt property from that moment on.

Mr. Williford left our hotel room, but returned in about an hour carrying a pistol. He headed directly to H.L. Hunt to kill him. Without hesitation, I was able to throw Mr. Williford to the floor and forcibly take the weapon from him.

After I had disarmed him, I was told by Mr. Hunt to take Mr. Williford to the airport and stay there until his airplane departed.

I called the Dallas office and advised them that H.L. Williford was not to be allowed into Hunt offices for any reason at any time.

After a few months, the two H.L.s began talking and seeing each other again, and I never heard of any further problem such as the one I witnessed in New York at the Waldorf-Astoria.

I have always kept the pistol that I took from Mr. Williford that day. The gun is described as an Iver Johnson Cadet and has the inscription "IJA8C WKS Fitchburg, Mass. U.S.A."

The gun I took from H.L. Williford. I still have it to this day.

The Frank Erickson Story

This story doesn't directly involve Mr. Hunt but is very indicative of the kinds of things that happened to me in his employ.

In the mid-1960s, H.L. Hunt was very active in making and placing money bets in most sporting events – especially football and horseracing. During this time, Frank Erickson from New York was the dean of all bookmakers. I made frequent trips to New York to either carry money to pay off losses or to pick up money won from a sports bet.

Mr. Erickson and I talked quite frequently on the telephone and discussed a variety of subjects. I had recently purchased a tract of land for Mr. Hunt located

67

about ninety miles east of El Paso, Texas. This tract of property was known as Indian Hot Springs. The six-hundred acres surrounding the land had an unbelievable number of wild quail – a hunter could get his bag limit in just a few minutes.

In one of my talks with Mr. Erickson, I began to talk about the quail in the Indian Hot Springs area. I told him I was coming to New York and if he wanted me to, I would bring him some "Texas quail." Mr. Hunt owed Erickson $400,000 on a gambling debt, and a Las Vegas gambler owed Mr. Hunt $800,000 on another bet, so I was going to New York to try to negotiate a deal to transfer the Las Vegas debt to Mr. Erickson and settle what Mr. Hunt owed.

At this time the FBI apparently had a telephone tap on Mr. Erickson's line, and for some reason, my offer to bring some "Texas quail" to New York got mistaken by the Feds that I was going to bring some young girls to New York for Erickson.

I did actually go to New York, where I planned to meet with Mr. Erickson and give him the two dozen quail packed in dry ice. I left Dallas on a flight and was scheduled to arrive in New York around 5:00 pm. The airplane only had about seven people on it as passengers – myself, a middle-aged couple, and four separate young ladies each traveling by herself. As far as I could tell, none of the people had a relationship with any of the others, except for the married couple, of course.

We landed in New York, and as I left the airplane, there were two men dressed in suits and ties that approached me and the four single ladies. The men identified themselves as FBI agents and instructed all of us to follow them to a nearby office. When we arrived, they immediately demanded to know the background on each of us and the relationship that I had with the four women. Of course, there was no relationship at all – we had simply all booked the same flight and did not even speak to each other on the plane.

When the FBI agents were finally satisfied that these ladies weren't the "quail" that I was bringing to Mr. Erickson, they let us go. I have often wondered what they thought of that Sunday afternoon flight incident... and I made a mental note to myself to be aware of future conversations that I had with Mr. Erickson on the phone.

Mr. Hunt, the Gambler

When Mr. Hunt did an interview with *Playboy* magazine in 1966, the reporter asked about his gambling and Mr. Hunt said, "Well, I quit playing poker in 1921, and as far as I know, I was the best."

That little dodge on gambling was just for the public, however, because Mr. Hunt bet on card games, football, horses, and many other things over the course of his entire life. It was one of his genuine pleasures, and to be honest, he was good at it.

I have mentioned that Mr. Hunt owed Frank Erickson $400,000 on a gambling debt, and this wasn't something unusual. He loved to gamble, and gamble big.

A Las Vegas gambler named Johnny Drew was the manager and five-percent owner of the Stardust Resort and Casino on the world-famous Las Vegas Strip. He was also a veteran associate of Al Capone. Drew owed Mr. Hunt $800,000 from a bet, and so I was sent to Vegas to the Stardust to collect the money.

The Stardust Hotel and Casino

When I arrived at the Stardust, I introduced myself and was taken to Mr. Drew's office – it was very large, and had a desk in the middle with two chairs in front of it. He indicated that I should sit down in one of the chairs, which I did.

I explained to Johnny Drew who I was, who I represented, and why I was there. He just stared at me, and then reached under his desk. I know that he was pushing a signal button, because a door on the back wall opened and two huge men in suits walked into the room. They helped me out of my chair and escorted me all the way to the airport. That was one of the few times that I failed Mr. Hunt.

Like I said earlier, sometime later I flew to New York – when the Texas quail incident occurred – to see if Mr.

Erickson would take the $800,000 debt owed to Mr. Hunt in exchange for the $400,000 that Mr. Hunt owed him. I was unsuccessful at that as well; I suppose that Frank Erickson didn't relish the thought of collecting from Johnny Drew, either.

This is just an example of the level of gambling that Mr. Hunt did, no matter what he told *Playboy* magazine. He was even subpoenaed to appear before a federal grand jury in Terre Haute, Indiana, that was investigating big-time gambling in the country. One of the other people who had also been served was Zeppo Marx, of the famous Marx Brothers comedy team. I don't know about Zeppo, but Mr. Hunt was able to get out of the appearance... and it didn't slow down his gambling in the least.

The Adlai Stevenson Incident

In the early 1960s, Adlai Stevenson came to Dallas to test the political waters for his expected run for president. It seems that every person running for a high-profile political position would always come to the H.L. Hunt office with the expectation of meeting Mr. Hunt. Of course, most of these meetings were for the purpose of raising money.

Adlai Stevenson came into the Hunt offices uninvited and requested to see Mr. Hunt. When a person of some standing did come into our office he was brought to me for further handling.

Although Mr. Hunt was not a supporter of Adlai Stevenson, he did, in fact, come into my office and visit with Mr. Stevenson for a short while. They just had a general conversation and some exchange of ideas.

On the same day, but a little later a young man named Robert Hatfield came into the office and he also wanted to see Mr. Hunt. Hatfield was turned over to me. He just wanted to meet Mr. Hunt and to ask him to autograph his newly-purchased copy of *Alpaca*. Mr. Hunt did see him and sign his book, and made a nice comment in the autograph.

Later on, Hatfield saw Adlai Stephenson on a Dallas street and spat directly into his face This incident made the news immediately, and Mr. Hunt was very concerned – in no way did he want the police to find a copy of *Alpaca* that he had just personalized and autographed in Hatfield's possession. After all, Hatfield had just assaulted a man who was considering running for president.

Adlai Stephenson

I was therefore tasked with getting the book back. I had one of the young women working in our office call Hatfield and ask him to meet her in the hotel lounge where he was staying for a five o'clock drink. In the meantime, the bell captain – a long time friend – agreed to unlock Hatfield's door and give me the time to search for the book. He did that for me, and I found the book in Hatfield's hotel room. I took it and quickly left.

As I passed the lounge, I signaled the young lady who was distracting Hatfield, and she excused herself to go to the ladies' room and departed as well.

I never heard from or saw Hatfield again, and I never heard anything about Mr. Hunt and the autographed book being associated with him – Mr. Hunt got the book back, and avoided any possible bad publicity.

The Discovery Well Photograph

This could be one of my favorite stories about Mr. Hunt. Not only does it show how little he cared about personal publicity, but how much he cared about business as well. The best thing about it, though, is that it represents an inside joke that has lasted for years. I fear that if I don't tell it here, the story might not ever be told.

The famous Discovery Well photograph

The photograph of the Discovery Well in the East Texas Oil Field has been printed in magazines, newspapers, books, online, and is even displayed at the East Texas Oil Museum in Kilgore, Texas.

The three people that are always identified in the photograph are 1) Dad Joiner (wearing tie and hat), third from the left, shaking the hand of 2) geologist Doc Lloyd, with 3) H.L. Hunt (with cigar and hat), the third from the right.

The thing is, that is not H.L. Hunt. This photograph was sent to Hunt Oil and Mr. Hunt was asked to identify himself for some display or publicity that it was going to be used for. He examined it, shook his head, and said, "I'm not in that picture."

I asked if he was sure, and told him that he really needed to be in the photograph. He stared at it for a minute and finally said, "Okay, let's make me the fellow in the hat, third from the right." So that's what we told them. Through the years, that has been identified as H.L. Hunt more times than I can count. In reality, I seem to remember that the fellow in the picture was a druggist from Kilgore... but it certainly wasn't Mr. Hunt.

He didn't care about personal publicity, nor did he have the kind of pride that would make him stand his ground that he wasn't in the photo. By the same token, he knew that it would be a good business move if he was in it, so he went along with what they wanted – him to be in the picture.

Like I said before, I understand that this photograph is displayed at the East Texas Oil Museum in Kilgore, so if you happen to stop by there, don't forget to look for it.

You can smile to yourself when you see the caption, and know that it isn't really Mr. Hunt – he just picked someone out to sort of be his stand-in.

Mr. Hunt and Anti-Semitism

Mr. Hunt believed that Jews controlled Wall Street, banks, press, radio and TV, and therefore had great influence on the spread of communism in the United States. Because of his stand, he was often referred to as being anti-Semitic.

If, in fact, he was anti-Semitic, he did not like that description and denied that it was accurate.

Still, when the Federal Bureau of Investigation's H.L. Hunt file was made public through the Freedom of Information Act, it contained a quote from the oilman: "Hate publications and hate groups are difficult to define," said Hunt. "It is completely inadvisable that *Life Line* string along with a white-supremacy group, but *Life Line* would not want to declare war on them or espouse the opposition to a white-supremacy group. Life Line is not anti-Semitic, but inasmuch as there will be practically no Jews who fail to fight *Life Line*, *Life Line* is not due to carry the torch for them."

Later, trying to educate *Life Line* associate James Wayne Poucher to pretense. Hunt suggested that he praise a well-known Jew because then "*Life Line* would be given the credit of extolling and memorializing a Jew."

Even after his death, however, the anti-Semantic tag continued to haunt Mr. Hunt. In 2006, the Denver Post reported that H.L. Hunt would not let his children shop at Neiman Marcus because "the owners were Jews."

But no matter what Mr. Hunt personally believed, he did not want to be labeled as an anti-Semite. To that end, I drafted the following letter on his behalf and had copies of it reproduced and mailed to thousands of people throughout the U.S.

H. L. HUNT
1704 MAIN STREET
DALLAS 1, TEXAS

May 8, 1964

Mr. Joe K. Mahoney
Mahoney and Yocum
Attorneys at Law
Armstrong Building
Eldorado, Arkansas

Dear Mr. Mahoney:

Many people who do not like my stand on communism strangely charge that I am anti-Semitic. I am sure that since my attitude toward Jews is well known in the small cities in which I have lived or in which I have transacted a great deal of business, I would like to get the programs I am sending you in vast quantities in the hands of many Jews in your city who have known me for years.

In addition to LIFE LINE material, I am sending copies of three pieces carrying clippings beginning with the NEW YORK HERALD TRIBUNE's September 27, 1963, piece. I have reproduced and distributed throughout the nation tens of thousands of these three pieces and my activity in this respect has kept the crusade against Soviet anti-Semitism alive until it is about to become a successful world-wide movement.

These old-time friends are in position to deny the charges of anti-Semitism made against me and against LIFE LINE whenever they hear them.

They would, no doubt, be glad to have this material, as it supports what they already know about me and, as these charges which are frequently made against me and against LIFE LINE are a matter of national interest, the opinions of these long-time friends and acquaintances may soon be repeated nationwide.

With best wishes...

Constructively,

H. L. Hunt

H. L. Hunt

HLH:js
Enclosures

The May 8, 1964, Anti-Semitic Letter

Did the letter help his reputation? I honestly don't know, but it did help Mr. Hunt's feelings that we were doing everything possible to fight the anti-Semite opinion that people had about him and the *Life Line* program.

The 60 Minutes Interview

In the Spring of 1969, journalist Mike Wallace interviewed H.L. Hunt on the television show *60 Minutes*. The segment started with a helicopter shot zooming across Dallas' White Rock Lake and coming up on Hunt's Mount Vernon home – it was an extremely dramatic opening to the piece.

While it was an interesting interview that was actually very complimentary, in the course of the taping there was one particular question that raised a bit of national ire against Mr. Hunt. Mike Wallace innocently posed the question to him, "Is it true that you make one million dollars a week?"

Mr. Hunt drew back, a little indignant, and said, "I'd starve if I only made a million dollars a week!"

That particular statement caught the attention of the country, and we were deluged with anti-Hunt letters coming into the office. Some people wanted to kill him, others wanted money from him, and some just wanted to meet this man to see what kind of advantage they could gain.

I think that we received about five hundred letters in all. Some were very direct, others were subdued, but I kept one that particularly caught my attention. The language in it is a bit coarse, and for that I apologize, but this is the text followed by a copy of the actual handwritten letter:

Dear H.L. Hitler Hunt

Enjoy your last hours as a fascist-pig-fuckface billionaire. I am going to kill you, you plain-folksy prick bastard. People like you shouldn't live long enough to die.

$1 million a week & you'd starve – I hope you rot in hell. I am going to beat the shit out of your stinking, fucking, fascist body before I murder you.

– A human being

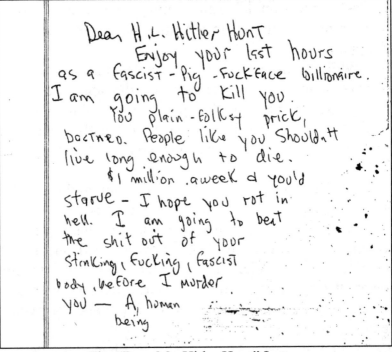

The "Dear Mr. Hitler Hunt" Letter

Most people would have considered the million-dollar statement that Mr. Hunt made in the interview to be a public relations disaster, but when it was all said and done, Mr. Hunt really didn't care what the public thought of him.

When you consider that fact, it's quite different from the celebrities of today's world who hire an army of publicists and spin doctors to keep their image pristine in the public eye.

But again, that was just Mr. Hunt.

Summing Up Mr. Hunt

I related all these stories not to entertain, amuse, or simply take up space in a book, but instead to present a perspective on H.L. Hunt that very few people have.

He was truly an enigma – on one hand, he lived in a larger-than-the-original version of George Washington's Mount Vernon, and had three chefs on staff to prepare dishes to order at every seated meal, yet on the other hand, he drove himself to work every day and carried his lunch in a brown paper bag.

He could afford designer clothes, but instead wore ordinary, off-the-rack suits. He once said, "If you know how rich you are, you aren't very rich."

Mr. Hunt could pick up the phone and directly call some of the most powerful men in the country – J. Edgar Hoover, Lyndon Baines Johnson, and Sam Rayburn, to name but a few.

There was literally nothing out of his reach, and that had been the case for so long that it would never occur to him to think otherwise… and that sets the stage for the motive and opportunity that he had to potentially be involved in four of the most significant murders of the twentieth century: John F. Kennedy, Martin Luther King, Robert F. Kennedy, and Jimmy Hoffa.

I'm certainly not saying that he planned those assassinations, and I don't have a smoking gun to reveal. Instead, I only have stories about events that went on surrounding them that involved Mr. Hunt, and I suspect that many people will find them as interesting as I do.

Now that you've had a bit of an exposure to Mr. Hunt, it's time to delve more deeply into the cases of those four men, their murders, and the events surrounding them.

H.L. Hunt's Mount Vernon, a near but larger replica in Dallas, Texas, of George Washington's Virginia estate home. (Carol M. Highsmith, photographer, Library of Congress)

Part III: Mr. Hunt and JFK

John F. Kennedy was being positioned by his family to sit in the biggest chair in the nation – the one in the White House Oval Office. Mr. Hunt was backing Lyndon Johnson from Hunt's home state of Texas for a number of reasons – not the least of which was the benevolent attitude that Johnson had toward Texas oil.

John F. Kennedy

Mr. Hunt was paying extremely close attention to the election, and that began a very interesting chain of events that would play out over the years that followed.

The 1960 Democratic National Convention

Everyone knew that the 1960 presidential election was going to be a horserace. The 34th president of the United States, Dwight D. Eisenhower, was finishing his second term in office and couldn't run again. Because the 22nd Amendment to the Constitution that prohibited a third term had been ratified in 1951, he was the first president in history to be constitutionally forbidden from seeking a third re-election.

The 1960 Democratic National Convention was held in Los Angeles, California, from July 11 through July 15, 1960, at the L.A. Memorial Sports Arena. The major players that were being considered for presidential nomination were Senator John F. Kennedy of Massachusetts, Governor Pat Brown of California, Senator Stuart Symington of Missouri, Senator Lyndon B. Johnson of Texas, former Illinois Governor Adlai Stevenson, Senator Wayne Morse of Oregon, and Senator Hubert Humphrey of Minnesota.

A number of the Democratic old guard favored Lyndon Johnson, including Sam Rayburn. At the time, Rayburn was arguably the most powerful man in Washington. He was Speaker of the House, an almost half-decade veteran of Congress, and a close friend and mentor of Johnson.

Lyndon Johnson himself wielded a good deal of power. He had served as a U.S. senator, the senate minority leader, senate majority whip, and the senate majority leader, and now had his eyes on the presidential nomination. Since Johnson was a fellow Texan, and he had supported oil depletion allowances for tax purposes – something that was very beneficial to oil men – Mr. Hunt felt like he was the best choice for the presidency. Not because he would be the man for the country as a whole, but because LBJ could do the best job for Hunt in the Oval Office.

Let me take a moment and explain that Mr. Hunt was not a Republican or a Democrat – he was for whichever candidate was going to be the best for his business. There are many times that I accompanied him to both conventions during an election year, and he was equally active at each one.

In 1960, Mr. Hunt and I flew out to Los Angeles so that he could stump for LBJ and also keep his eye on things. There was confidence in the air – both Rayburn and Johnson went into the convention knowing that they had the party under control and that LBJ would receive the nomination.

Mr. Hunt worked the convention, talking with delegates and visiting with party officials, and little by little it became unfortunately clear that his candidate was out, and that John Fitzgerald Kennedy was going to be in.

The 1960 Democratic National Convention

The other candidates were attacking various aspects of Kennedy's campaign. Some raised the question of his religion, pointing out that it would extremely difficult for a Catholic to carry the Protestant-heavy South. Others repeated the rumor that he was ill, suffering from Addison's disease, a long-term endocrine disorder. Still, others talked openly about his reputation as a playboy and womanizer.

Lyndon Baines Johnson

It was obvious, however, that in spite of JFK's rivals for the nomination, Joe Kennedy and Bobby Kennedy had control of the convention. Both were very active, while JFK kept a very low profile and spent most of the convention just having a good time. Mr. Hunt and I were told that he had a private bungalow where he was hiding out and that ladies were delivered there around the clock.

The Kennedys all disliked Lyndon Johnson and Johnson disliked the Kennedys, but it soon became clear that Johnson might be the one thing that the ticket needed to win the overall election. Johnson didn't want this, however, and neither did the Kennedys. Nevertheless, Joe, the patriarch of the family, called on H.L. Hunt to try to persuade Johnson to take the vice president position. They had a number of meetings to discuss the best way to accomplish this; as the convention progressed, the three most powerful men there were Joe Kennedy, his son Bobby, and H.L. Hunt.

Mr. Hunt did not have an easy task – LBJ had loud, profanity-ridden fits whenever the subject was broached. Nevertheless, Mr. Hunt began The United States dialogue with Johnson to convince him to accept the second spot. Hunt appealed to his ego, pointing out that he was a natural leader. He also explained the power that would be supporting him in the form of Sam Rayburn. Finally, Hunt pointed out that any number of things could happen to Kennedy in the course of four years: his health was rumored to be bad, he had the reputation as a womanizer, and he had a number of enemies in the party and beyond.

Finally, Mr. Hunt explained to Johnson that taking the second chair was the only way that he could eventually achieve the presidency. By doing so, he would get excellent exposure to the people of America and in 1964, could go for the presidential nomination.

I believe that Mr. Hunt had little to no confidence in JFK as a president or as a person. He probably felt like having Johnson waiting in the wings to take over the job – be it as a result of the next election, or in case something happened to Kennedy during his term – would be an asset.

There actually were any number of things that could derail the JFK presidency; there were the health rumors and his well-known womanizing to start with. Over the years, though, I've often wondered if there were other considerations that I simply wasn't privy to. No matter; Mr. Hunt badly wanted Lyndon Johnson in the second position, ready to step up. If LBJ could start working on a power base in Washington while he patiently waited out Kennedy, then all the better.

On the other hand, Bobby had the arduous task of convincing JFK to accept Johnson as his vice presidential candidate. John Kennedy did not want Johnson, nor did the majority of the delegates at the convention. They all finally accepted the fact, however, that LBJ could help carry the Southern states that were going to cause the most problems for John Kennedy.

Bobby Kennedy also assured his brother that Lyndon Johnson was only needed for the first term. After that, he was sure that he had enough information on LBJ and his adviser Bobby Baker to indict both of them before the end of John's first term in office.

Mr. Hunt had hoped that Johnson would be able to establish a power base as the vice president that would catapult him into the presidency in 1964.After the election when Kennedy and Johnson moved into their new positions, however, just the opposite occurred. Lyndon Johnson's influence slipped more and more every day.

Dr. Crisswell's Sermon

H.L. Hunt played a vital role at the 1960 Democratic Convention in securing the nomination for John F. Kennedy, and for securing the VP spot for Lyndon Johnson.

After the nominations, both JFK and LBJ were on the campaign trail. JFK with his good looks and background was very popular, but most people considered that the final vote would be very close – LBJ offered little benefit. Little did they know, Mr. Hunt was working on a scheme to help launch the ticket into the White House.

Mr. Hunt was a member of the First Baptist Church in Dallas (the largest Baptist church in the world) and was good friends with its pastor Dr. W.A. Criswell – at this time, it was well known that Dr. Criswell was the best, most respected non-Catholic religious leader in the United States.

Both JFK and LBJ had been crisscrossing the U.S. to express their views and get votes. H.L. Hunt came up with an unusual, and I think unbelievable, idea. To begin implementing it, he called Dr. Criswell and told him that I was going to meet him to present an idea that would be most effective in the 1960 presidential race.

I went to Dr. Criswell's Office at the downtown First Baptist Church and discussed Mr. Hunt's plan. In this plan, Dr. Criswell was to deliver a sermon in his Sunday morning service that would denounce both the Catholic Church and John F. Kennedy. In this sermon, Criswell would outline in detail the influence that the Roman Catholic Church would have on the U.S. through JFK and how the Protestant citizens of the country would be damaged by this. The sermon would also present the idea that as president, John F. Kennedy would be subject to a heavy influence by the Vatican to carry out the Church's agenda in America, even against the U.S. citizens.

Dr. Criswell and I visited about an hour and a half and he said, "John, I like the idea – it is exactly what I think and believe. It has to be done." Before I left his office, the pastor asked me to do a favor for a member of his family who had some personal problems. Who and what it was is not important, and is therefore not worth mentioning here; I told him that I would take care of his request, which I did.

The sermon was delivered by Dr. Criswell at 10:50 am on July 3, 1960. The entire transcript of the sermon has been reproduced many times over the years and is readily available online, and it bears close examination. Dr.

Criswell started out the sermon by saying, "Now the sermon this morning has governmental overtones, and I do not want to hold you here under a false pretense as though you had come to listen to a sermon, and I deliver a political address. So I am going to give you an opportunity to leave – anybody that would like to leave. We are going to sing a hymn written by a great Baptist preacher, and we are going to sing the first and the last stanzas of it without a book. And while we sing that song, anybody that would like to leave is privileged to do so; you are not going to hear a sermon this morning. You are going to hear an address, and it has, as I say, tremendous governmental overtones. And I am not asking you to stay; you are at liberty to leave. Now let's sing this Baptist hymn dedicated to our country. Let's stand. (singing) My country, 'tis of thee, sweet land of liberty…"

There are a couple of interesting things about this. The first of which is that by uttering those words about an address with governmental overtones from the pulpit, Dr. Criswell was jeopardizing the tax exempt status of one of the largest Baptist Churches in the world. The Internal Revenue Code clearly prohibits intervention in political campaigns by organizations that are exempt from federal income tax under section 501(c)(3), which includes religious organizations. It could be that Dr. Criswell knew he was one of the most powerful Protestant ministers in the country, and therefore thought himself untouchable. On the other hand, since the request for the sermon came from Mr. Hunt, he could have also assumed that Hunt had the power to protect him from the nuisance of any accusation or prosecution.

The other thing that is interesting is that he put the congregation in a precarious situation. He told them that it would be a political talk and that they could leave if they wanted to, but to do so, they would have to walk out of the sanctuary during the singing of the patriotic American anthem, *My Country 'Tis of Thee*. I can't imagine a lot of people wanting their friends and fellow parishioners seeing them do that. By starting his sermon that way, he more or less had a captive audience.

Dr. Criswell went on to attack Kennedy and his Catholic religion directly, saying, "In November of 1957, Senator John Kennedy stated, 'People are afraid that Catholics take orders from a higher organization. They don't, or at least I don't.' And he continues that and continues that and continues that. Now, as Senator Kennedy continued in this avowal, in May of this year, 1960, the official newspaper of the Vatican, *L'Osservatore Romano*, published a special article, which is labeled 'authoritatively binding on all the church.' It said, and I quote from the officially published editorial of the Vatican paper, 'The church has full powers of true jurisdiction over all the faithful, and hence has the duty and the right to guide, direct, and correct them on the plane of action and ideas. The church has the duty and the right to intervene even in the political field, to enlighten and help consciences. A Catholic can never prescind the teachings and directives of the church. In every section of his activities, he must inspire his private and public conduct by the laws, orientation, and instructions of the hierarchy.' End quote. And that was published in order that John Kennedy himself might know that his avowals that, 'I can be disassociated from and free from the claims

89

of the Roman Catholic Church,' the hierarchy says, 'It is not so.' Now immediately that created a tremendous repercussion here in America, and the following is an editorial comment in the current home mission magazine of our Southern Baptist Convention: the United States Catholic officials immediately began to say that this pronouncement of the Vatican did not apply here. No, of course not. Neither does the Catholic Church close Baptist churches in the United States, as it closes Baptist churches in Spain. But once given the power to do so without strong opposition, then what is the Catholic position?"

Dr. Criswell was making a strong case to his congregation that should a Catholic president be elected, they would be subject to the control of the Roman Catholic Church. But if that wasn't strong enough, he ended the sermon with a direct shot over the bow of JFK's campaign:

"The Roman Church wins most of its victories with the weapon of time. Kennedy, in today, with strong emphasis that he says on separation of church and state; and the door is open for another Catholic leader who gives the Pope, his ambassador, the church schools state support; and finally, recognition of one church above America. Then religious liberty has also died in America, as it has died in Spain, as it has died in Columbia, as it has died wherever the Roman Catholic hierarchy has the ableness and the power to shut it down and to destroy it in death."

When it was over, Dr. Criswell had done what Mr. Hunt had wanted. The sermon was recorded on tape, which I picked up after the service. I went directly to our office and had the words transcribed. I left Dallas the next

90

morning, which was Monday, with the written version of the sermon and $200,000 in cash. I had located a company in New York that had the name and address of every Protestant minister in the U.S. and other parts of the world.

I had about 200,000 copies made; each was stuffed into a plain envelope and sent out to the mailing list to all those Protestant pastors. I did not include my name or address as the sender; I didn't know at the time that my failure to do so violated a federal law which required that the sender must be identified by name and address when the material is mailed concerning anyone running for president.

On one Saturday morning about twenty days later two FBI agents came into my office. They identified themselves and advised me of my rights not to answer their questions.

The agents told me why they were there – that I had violated the law and that I could be charged with over 200,000 separate illegal acts.

We had a very short visit – I gave no answers to their questions. I instead told the agents that I needed an attorney present at our next meeting, if in fact there was a next meeting. Within a week of that encounter, my Criswell-mailing story was on every radio and TV station, and in every newspaper. At that time, H.L. Hunt had been identified as the person responsible for the mailing, and we learned that both Mr. Hunt and myself were going to be subpoenaed to appear before a Senate committee that could and would file federal charges against the two of us.

Inasmuch as we were both easy to locate, and inasmuch as the both of us had left a broad paper trail, our only avenue at that time was to go underground and disappear.

I left Dallas for a three month period of time – I traveled under the name of "John Core" and spent most of my time just traveling the region: South Texas, New Mexico, Oklahoma, and Arkansas. I kept up with my court and news activity as almost every day there was a story on some news outlet about this event.

Mr. Hunt sought anonymous refuge in an apartment building owned by his daughter on Preston Road in Dallas called Behind the Pink Wall Apartments. Both Mr. Hunt and I avoided being caught, arrested, and going to jail... although there was one particular day that frightened us both.

I was with Mr. Hunt in the apartment where he was hiding out, and simultaneously there was a knock on the front and back door. We looked at each other, both realizing that we'd been caught. After a moment of standing there in silence, I said, "Well, let's get this over with."

I walked to the back door and opened it, fully expecting to be face-to-face with an FBI agent, but instead, I saw a woman standing there. She introduced herself as a neighbor and explained that she was doing some baking and just discovered that she was out of sugar. She didn't want to stop what she was doing and go to the store and asked if she could borrow some from me. I was happy to get her what she needed, a little shocked that I wasn't in handcuffs.

When she left, I shut the door and gave Mr. Hunt a "we dodged a bullet on that one" look and went to see what was going on at the front door. When I opened it, the newspaper boy was there to collect for the month, and I was just as stunned with that as I was with the lady and the sugar. I paid him, shut the door, and shook my head. I had been sure that we were caught, but instead, it had simply been a coincidence.

Mr. Hunt's original theory on this mailing that had so much potential trouble for us was that a story against the Roman Catholic Church would unite the Catholics and that the Protestant preachers who received the sermon would take disfavor against Criswell for such poor taste in mailing his sermon. In H.L. Hunt's mind, he considered this simple act to be the most important press coverage ever exposed to would-be voters and was important in JFK and LBJ winning the 1960 presidential race.

With the wide coverage to which this story was exposed, it is my opinion and the opinion of others that this simple event provided widespread coverage to the presidential race, and was the single most important factor in the presidential election.

At the same time that I made the Dr. Criswell mailing, a one-page (front and back) sheet was written outlining all of the positive points of Lyndon Johnson – it was a very favorable story and one that LBJ was proud of. I employed about fifty part-time ladies who mailed a copy of this one-page Johnson story to each person with the name of "Johnson" whose listing appeared in the telephone books of major cities. We worked out of the Dallas Library, as the library had a number of out of town phone books. For other cities that we were interested in, I would call someone that I knew in those cities and have a copy of their telephone book sent to me.

I have no idea how many "Johnson" stories we mailed out. I would put the total figure in the 300,000 range. This mailing process took about thirty days and quite a bit of money. We were praising Johnson in this mailing and very negative against Kennedy and the Criswell sermon. All of this was banking on the fact that someone named "Johnson" would take a favorable look at a candidate with the same surname. What effect it actually had, I'll never know.

The account of Criswell's sermon has been told a number of times in books and in the media. From the time that it first happened up until today, there are still references made in the media to this unusual sermon presentation. Yet, I have not seen one story about it that has been able to express the real reason behind the entire event. It was never Mr. Hunt's intent to use the copies of the sermon against Kennedy; in fact, just the opposite was true. H.L. Hunt was thinking like a chess grandmaster, planning several moves ahead in the game.

He knew that a widespread release of the sermon would 1) cause those in the Catholic faith to unite in support of Kennedy; and 2) most of the 200,000 Protestant ministers who received a copy would reject the Criswell message and would cast a cloud on anyone who would dare deliver a political message from the pulpit.

The endgame for Mr. Hunt was very simple: to get Lyndon Baines Johnson into the White House. As he learned at the Democratic National Convention, the road to that happening could only begin with the JFK/LBJ ticket winning the election.

RFK and LBJ

On October 26, 1997, the *New York Times* wrote about the uneasy relationship, saying, "The feud began in 1960, when Robert Kennedy directed his brother John's successful campaign for the Democratic presidential nomination. The main competitor, Johnson, the Senate majority leader, raised not only the 'Catholic issue' but also the health problems of John F. Kennedy, who spent much of the 50s recovering from delicate spinal surgery and who had Addison's disease, an adrenal malfunction that required daily doses of cortisone. As the convention neared, Johnson described his now-robust opponent as a 'little scrawny fellow with rickets' and other unnamed maladies. The Kennedy camp whispered about the lingering effects of Johnson's 1955 heart attack."

Robert Kennedy and LBJ

Commenting on the relationship, in 1997 the *New York Times* reported, "In 1961, at a late-night supper in the White House living quarters, Vice President Lyndon B. Johnson accosted Attorney General Robert F. Kennedy in front of embarrassed friends and officials. 'Bobby, you do not like me,' Johnson declared. 'Your brother likes me. Your sister-in-law likes me. Your daddy likes me. But you don't like me. Now, why? Why don't you like me?' Kennedy did not respond to Johnson that evening, but his feelings were clear."

In 1964 Jacqueline Kennedy gave an oral interview about her husband and his presidency that was sealed for fifty years. When it was finally made public a few years ago, Jackie gave some insight into the RFK-LBJ relationship. She said, "Bobby told me this later, and I know Jack said it to me sometimes. He said, 'Oh, God, can you ever imagine what would happen to the country if Lyndon was president?'"

Jackie went on to say, "He [JFK] didn't like that idea that Lyndon would go on and be president because he was worried for the country. Bobby told me that he'd had some discussions with him. I forget exactly how they were planning or who they had in mind. It wasn't Bobby, but somebody. Do something to name someone else in '68."

All this was substantiated by JFK's secretary Evelyn Lincoln, who wrote a book in 1968 titled, *Kennedy and Johnson*. She noted that on November 19, 1963, the president told her, "You know, if I am reelected in '64, I am going to spend more and more time making government service an honorable career. I am going to advocate changing some of the outmoded rules and regulations in Congress, such as the seniority rule. To this,

I will need as a running mate in sixty-four a man who believes as I do." He added, "It is too early to make an announcement about another running mate – that will perhaps wait until the convention."

When Evelyn Lincoln asked about his choice of a running mate, the president replied, "At this time I am thinking about Governor Terry Sanford of North Carolina. But it will not be Lyndon."

I don't have a single doubt in my mind that Lyndon Johnson knew that he was out in 1964. Unless there was some radical change or some unforeseen event, his political life would soon be over.

Life Line and JFK

If Mr. Hunt had a part in the assassination of President John F. Kennedy, it wasn't with a 6.5×52mm Carcano Model 91/38 infantry rifle. No, that was Oswald's weapon of choice. Instead, Mr. Hunt was involved with something that would seem very benign to most people but was instead very, very powerful: a national radio program.

For a greater appreciation of this book, the reader needs to have an understanding of the H.L. Hunt's *Life Line* radio show. You see, in the 1950s, Mr. Hunt's interest turned to politics. He became concerned – if not downright consumed – with the threat of liberals and communism, so he started an educational foundation called *Facts Forum* in 1951.

It was the job of *Facts Forum* to distribute anticommunist, pro-American information using many forms of media: radio, television, pamphlets, and books. By 1956 he had poured $3.5 million into the organization.

Facts Forum was not without its detractors, however. Journalists and government officials had begun to question how such an obviously political organization was being allowed to pass as an educational nonprofit. Although he didn't want to, Mr. Hunt suspended the operation of *Facts Forum* in 1956.

Two years later, H.L. Hunt re-launched his conservative agenda with a radio program called *Life Line*.

Life Line was a seven-day-a-week, 15-minute radio program that was first broadcast on November 10, 1958. Throughout the 1960s era, it was aired on over 500 radio stations around the country and was followed by an estimated five million people. This daily exposure enabled listeners to tune in almost any time of day, anywhere in the U.S. to hear the *Life Line* message on one radio station or another.

When describing *Life Line*, *Texas Monthly* magazine wrote, "The guiding principle of *Life Line* is anti-communism, and it is delivered in fire and brimstone sermons about the evils of everything that has transpired since Sherman rode through Georgia and Roosevelt sold out at Yalta. The sum of it seems to have given form to some of the heart of darkness and fear of change that is in us all. The foe is everywhere, subversive and conspiratorial, and the instinct is to stack rifles in the basement and vote against minorities and longhairs and the welfare state."

The cost for H.L. Hunt to purchase airtime from radio stations for the program was around $6,000 cash every single day. In addition to radio time charges, *Life Line* maintained two separate offices in both Washington, D.C., and Dallas, Texas. Those offices were equipped with complete administrative staff, professional writers, recording studios, tape and record producing facilities, engineers and speakers.

Life Line was developed, produced and distributed by H.L. Hunt as a vehicle for him to express his political views and to expose those in public life who did not accept Mr. Hunt's political views. After all, the *Life Line* message was Mr. Hunt's message.

He believed that by continually broadcasting this message via *Life Line*, he could cause millions of people to join his crusade. After all, listeners were being exposed to daily suggestions... and Mr. Hunt felt that listeners would take whatever steps were necessary to correct an unfavorable situation.

At some time, almost anyone that was a *Life Line* supporter should have stopped and asked three questions: 1) who is presenting *Life Line*, 2) what is its purpose, 3) what is expected in return for the millions and millions of dollars being spent?

The answer to those questions was simple. Mr. Hunt believed that if he would broadcast his message on a daily basis in an educational talk radio program, the vast majority of the dedicated listeners would take care of anyone who did not share the *Life Line* view. They would either vote them out of office or remove them from public recognition by some other method.

Life Line was an anti-communist, pro-American, right-wing, conservative program dedicated to exposing those with any opposing views. It was H.L. Hunt's mission that *Life Line* would be the vehicle to attract many listeners to accept his views and beliefs.

One of the targets of *Life Line* was a young congressman from Massachusetts named John Fitzgerald Kennedy. The congressman had his eye on the presidency, which was a problem for Mr. Hunt. Not only was Kennedy a Catholic in a mostly-Protestant nation, but he had the reputation of being a playboy with an interest in the ladies instead of business.

More than that, however, was the fact that Kennedy was no friend to the giant oil barons. Mr. Hunt and others felt that not only would JFK close certain tax loopholes that were very beneficial to them, but that he was going to reduce the oil depletion allowance, a tax write-off that allowed them to keep 27.5% of their oil revenue tax-free. Should this allowance be reduced or completely taken away, *World Petroleum* magazine estimated that it could cost the industry as much as $280 million in annual profits.

During one of the 1960 Kennedy-Nixon debates, this particular question was put forth. The moderator asked, "Oilmen in Texas are seeking assurance from Senator Johnson that the oil depletion allowance will not be cut. Do you consider the 27.5% depletion allowance inequitable?"

John Kennedy replied, "There are about one hundred and four commodities that have some kind of depletion allowance – different kind of minerals, including oil. I believe all of those should be gone over in detail to make sure that no one is getting a tax break. That includes oil; it includes all kinds of minerals; it includes everything within the range of taxation. It includes oil abroad. I have voted in the past to reduce the depletion allowance for the largest producers; for those from $5 million dollars down, to maintain it at 27.5%."

The largest producers that Kennedy mentioned, which included Mr. Hunt, saw this not only as a bad business break but potentially as downright robbery. They would lose millions, if not billions of dollars collectively.

As President Kennedy was preparing for his Dallas visit in 1963, Mr. Hunt was putting millions of dollars into an anti-Kennedy radio campaign through his *Life Line* program. *Life Line* was continuing to broadcast its anti-Kennedy message, mercilessly attacking what the program called "the mistaken," the moniker that *Life Line* gave the president's supporters.

The program warned that Kennedy was bypassing the laws of Congress, following communist policies right out of Moscow, going against politicians who spoke out for American freedom and using taxpayer funds to subsidize communism all across the globe.

Life Line also attacked Kennedy's support of Medicare for elderly healthcare. It cautioned its listeners that the government would set up death panels to decide who lives and who dies, saying that Medicare was "a package which would literally make the president of the United States a medical czar with potential life-or-death power over every man, woman, and child in the country."

In his book *Kingdom: The Story of the Hunt Family of Texas*, author Jerome Tuccille noted, "In the weeks preceding his arrival, *Life Line* became increasingly strident in its anti-Kennedy rhetoric. Commentators on the program accused the president of every unpatriotic crime imaginable, from circumventing the authority of Congress to being a willing puppet of international communism. On

101

the morning of November 22, 1963, the day of Kennedy's scheduled arrival, *Life Line* went on the air with a dire warning to the people of America. The commentator started off by talking about the 'leftist plot,' fomented in Washington under the current administration, to deprive the people of their right to bear arms. 'In a dictatorship,' the broadcast continued, 'no firearms are permitted to the people, because they would then have the weapons with which to rise up against their oppressors.'"

The Attempt on General Edwin Walker

In 1963, retired army General Edwin A. Walker was living in Dallas and was becoming well known as a strong vocal spokesman for the same political messages that were being presented by H.L. Hunt.

I do not know if you could say Hunt and Walker were good friends, but you could certainly say they were both known for their outspoken views and right-wing conservative political ideals.

Walker had served in both World War II and the Korean War, and he was highly decorated during his service. Among other accolades and honors, he had been awarded the Bronze Star, the Legion of Merit, and the Silver Star.

General Walker would come into my office from time to time, and usually, Mr. Hunt would stroll in and join us for a ten or fifteen-minute visit.

The reason that General Walker came by was for information. You see, Mr. Hunt's *Life Line* radio program was on a daily schedule presenting the same right-wing views as those espoused by General Walker, so he wanted to get information. It was a win/win for Mr. Hunt because

Walker provided another avenue to disperse his agenda. Over a long period of time, I furnished General Walker with a lot of background material that we used in the *Life Line* radio program.

General Walker had been doing some public speaking, and he was also publishing a newsletter that expressed the same stories and ideas as those presented by *Life Line*. In other words, the material used by General Walker was the same material used in the *Life Line* broadcasts. Words had been changed and rearranged in the newsletter, but the political theme was the same.

On April 10, 1963, General Walker was enjoying a relaxing evening in the study of his Dallas home. A shot rang out, and a bullet came through the window frame and hit the wall near the general. Thankfully, his only injury was when splinters went into his forearm.

Although the police had no leads in the attempted murder, they released an official statement that said, "Whoever shot at the general was playing for keeps. The sniper wasn't trying to scare him. He was shooting to kill."

I continued to supply Walker with information that he used in his talks and such, and Mr. Hunt and I would even visit in his home occasionally. One night when we were there – and this was before the Kennedy assassination – Walker said that a suspect named Oswald had been mentioned as General Walker's would-be killer.

General Edwin Walker

103

Clearly, the police, and perhaps even the FBI, had Oswald on their radar at least for that shooting.

After President Kennedy was assassinated, Marina Oswald spent weeks being interrogated by the FBI. One of the stories that she told them was that on the evening of the attempted murder of General Walker, her husband had gone out, but he left a handwritten note in Russian with instructions as to what she was to do if he was arrested. Later that evening, he came home and told her that he had taken the shot at General Walker but had missed.

I believe that the forensic examination determined that the bullet could have come from the same gun that Oswald used to shoot Kennedy, but it could not be conclusively proven. Nevertheless, both the FBI and the Warren Commission determined that Oswald had fired the shot at General Walker some seven months before killing Kennedy.

I will always regret that I did not devote more time to the Oswald–Walker shooting. Could Oswald have had the same thought on why these two men should have both been killed? I don't know the answer, and I don't think that anyone ever will. It just seems odd that Oswald would shoot Walker who had from time to time denounced Kennedy, and then turn around and shoot Kennedy himself.

The Meeting That Never Was

I am not inclined to spend a lot of time commenting on all of the various conspiracy theories about the assassination of John F. Kennedy that have been floating around for years. There is, however, one thing that my name has been repeatedly associated with, and I feel that I should probably take a moment to set the record straight.

There was a woman who claimed to be LBJ's girlfriend and part of a very elite group. She said in both print interviews and on television shows that the night before the assassination of John Kennedy, she was attending a party with Johnson at the Dallas home of oilman Clint Murchison.

According to her, the guest list was a regular "who's who" of the day, including Murchison, FBI Director J. Edgar Hoover, Associate FBI Director (and rumored romantic partner to Hoover) Clyde Tolson, banker and Washington player John J. McCloy, former Vice President and Congressman Richard Nixon, Vice President Lyndon Johnson, Houston construction magnate George Brown, Dallas nightclub owner Jack Ruby, H.L. Hunt, and Hunt's right-hand man, yours truly, John Curington. I've seen the guest list vary depending on who's relating the account, but those are the major players that seem to usually be named.

The alleged lady friend of LBJ contends that once all the players had arrived, the men retired behind closed doors for a meeting. According to her account, when the meeting was over, LBJ came up to her and said, "After tomorrow those goddamn Kennedys will never embarrass me again. That's no threat. That's a promise."

The only problem with her story is that the meeting never happened. I never went to such a gathering. I can also say with a high degree of certainty that Mr. Hunt did not attend, either. If he had gone to Murchison's house, there's simply no question that he would have asked me to drive over with him. Not only did I accompany him almost everywhere, but I knew almost every minute of his daily schedule.

More than that, however, there are people on the guest list that would never have been in the same room with each other. Jack Ruby is probably the most obvious. He was a wannabe gangster at best, so even if he was going to be used as part of some plot or conspiracy, he would never have been asked to be part of the planning stage with some of the most powerful men in the world. Personally, I doubt that Jack Ruby could have even found his way to the house.

As far as I know, Mr. Hunt never met – or even saw – the woman telling this tale. I met her only once when she showed up at my ranch to ask me to confirm several of her stories. I would not do so, because as far as I could tell, they were simply untrue, just like the one about the meeting.

Don't get me wrong… this "covert planning meeting" makes an incredibly wonderful story, and if there was even a small grain of truth to it, I would have been foolish not to open this book with it. It never happened, however, probably to the disappointment of many people who study the JFK assassination. Again, this is my story of the alleged events, but it is my opinion that there was no such meeting at Mr. Murchison's house. I was not there, Mr. Hunt was not there, and based on my knowledge of the other people on the list, neither was anyone else. Should such a meeting have occurred, several of the people on the supposed list would have notified Mr. Hunt that they were in Dallas.

Assassination Day

President Kennedy's November 1963 visit to Dallas had been widely publicized. It seemed to be in all of the newspapers and on every channel of the television. The trip had been announced two months before, and the motorcade route had been released a few days before his arrival.

Kennedy spent November 22nd in Fort Worth, and even though the weather was rainy, thousands of people had turned out to greet him. He and the First Lady spent the night at the Hotel Texas there in town.

The morning of the 22nd Kennedy made a speech before taking Air Force One from Carswell Air Force Base to Love Field in Dallas. Later, the nation learned that presidential aide Kenneth O'Donnell had told the Secret Service that the bubble top for the president's limousine should be removed if it was not raining.

The presidential airplane touched down at Love Field at 11:39 am, and the motorcade left just a few minutes before noon, heading for the Dallas Business and Trade Mart where the president would make another speech, and then attend a steak dinner for local city leaders.

People had lined the streets to catch a glimpse of the president and his entourage as they passed by.

Mr. Hunt and I stepped over to one of the seventh-floor windows in our office at the Mercantile Bank Building and watched the motorcade as it headed down Main Street. Mr. Hunt didn't comment on it, but as the presidential limousine passed, I remember Governor Connally looking up. He certainly knew where Mr. Hunt's office was, and I assume that he was looking to see if anyone was watching. The Governor must have seen us there because he turned and said something to Kennedy, who looked up and waved as they went by. I guess not even the president of the United States could resist acknowledging the world's richest man. They disappeared from sight, and Mr. Hunt and I went back to our desks.

I received a phone call within a few minutes and was told, "There have been shots fired at the president." My first thought was that it would have been impossible. After all, I'd just seen the president moments before. Still, I reported this to Mr. Hunt, who paid no attention to it at all.

President Kennedy's motorcade

Back in my office I turned on my television and soon saw that JFK had indeed been shot. It wasn't long after that we learned that the president had been declared dead at 1:00 pm in Parkland Hospital's Trauma Room One.

Later, I learned that LBJ had insisted on being sworn in on Air Force One before takeoff back to Washington. In an ironic twist, they didn't have a Bible, so he put his hand on a Catholic Missal, which is a book that has all the instructions and texts necessary for the celebration of mass throughout the year. It was already on the plane in the bedroom's nightstand, probably a gift from someone to President Kennedy, because it was still in its cellophane wrapper.

After taking the oath of office, adding the words "So help me God" that are not part of the oath, the new president kissed his wife, shook hands all around, and then gave his very first executive order. Although I've heard more sanitized versions, my understanding is that Johnson declared, "Let's get this goddamn thing airborne."

A few years later when Mr. Hunt was being interviewed by *Playboy* magazine, he said, "The United Press quoted Senator Maurine Neuberger a few minutes after the assassination to the effect that if anyone is responsible for the assassination, it is H.L. Hunt of Dallas, Texas. Well, soon after that, my house phone began receiving a few friendly calls of warning and many threatening calls to the effect that I would be shot next, and also to tell Mrs. Hunt she would be shot. My office force would not consent to either of us going home even to get our clothes. We were sent out of town, and neither the police department nor the FBI would consent to us returning to Dallas until a few days before Christmas."

To be honest, I think that was just Mr. Hunt giving a fanciful story to the reporter. He actually got more death threats after Martin Luther King was assassinated than he did for JFK. Still, it wouldn't be hard for someone to call him at home – his number was listed right there in the telephone directory along with everyone else's. I guess that there were enough calls that he stayed at his home, Mount Vernon, for a while and tried not to be too much of a public figure. He came into the office occasionally and might have even taken a trip to New York with his wife where he always stayed at the Waldorf-Astoria. So he did tone down his public appearances. By no means, however, did he go into deep hiding after the assassination. That just didn't happen.

One thing that we did do was to assemble a team of secretaries to call all of the radio stations that aired *Life Line* and advise them not to air any more programs that mentioned John F. Kennedy – this would help distance *Life Line* and Mr. Hunt from the situation.

I have been told that his daughter, Swanee, was being so harassed with accusations of her father's part in the assassination of the president that years later, she had to temporarily leave Southern Methodist University. Perhaps the fallout from the rumors had long-term effects on Mr. Hunt's family as well.

Meanwhile, Lee Harvey Oswald had been arrested and was in the custody of the Dallas Police Department. At one point when the cameras were on him, Oswald looked at a reporter and said three words that have gone down in history: "I'm a patsy!"

The Murder of Lee Harvey Oswald

On Saturday afternoon, November 23, 1963, the nation was in shock over the death of the president two days earlier. Late that afternoon, I got a call from a lady who did cleaning and ironing for my family. She said that her husband had been arrested for a DWI, and she asked me to get him out of jail so that he could come home.

Before I could leave, the phone rang again – it was about 5:30 pm or so. When I picked it up, Mr. Hunt asked me to go down to the police station and check out what kind of security, if any, they had around Lee Harvey Oswald. I never questioned anything that Mr. Hunt asked me to do, and with the DWI case, I had a perfect excuse to be in and around the police station.

Bonding someone out of a DWI required maneuvering back and forth between the police station and the courthouse, so I went into the police station three separate times. No one questioned me, checked my credentials, searched my briefcase, or took any special security measures. In fact, on one of my visits, I pushed the elevator button and when it opened up, Captain Will Fritz was standing there with Oswald in handcuffs. Obviously, he was being moved around for questioning or some other reason. Captain Fritz recognized me and said, "Meet the son-of-a-bitch who killed the president!" I had seen Oswald before, and so I made no comment.

When I finished with the DWI, I went home and phoned Mr. Hunt about midnight. He had been very specific in his instructions that I was to call him no matter how late it was. I told him about my experience at the police station, and I assured him that there was no extraordinary security around Oswald at all. Mr. Hunt then asked me to contact Joe Civello, the head of the Dallas organized crime family and ask him to stop by

111

Mount Vernon (the Hunt home) because Mr. Hunt wanted to talk to him. Civello did so about 6:00 am on Sunday.

Later that morning, I was sitting at the First Baptist Church of Dallas listening to a sermon by Dr. W.A. Criswell when someone walked over and handed him a piece of paper. He opened it, read it, and after a pause, somberly announced, "Lee Harvey Oswald has just been shot."

I had a sick feeling in the pit of my stomach and thought about my visit to the jail to check on security and my contacting Joe Civello.

I later learned the details. At 11:21 am, Oswald was being transferred to the county jail by armored car. As he was being taken through the basement of the police station, Dallas nightclub owner Jack Ruby pulled out a gun and shot him in the gut. About two hours later, Oswald would die at Parkland Hospital – the same facility where President Kennedy had been taken two days before.

There have been many different theories as to what prompted Jack Ruby to shoot Lee Harvey Oswald. What I know about Ruby was that he was a wannabe gangster that ran a burlesque club in Dallas. He badly wanted to be someone important but never was.

Mr. Hunt was aware of who Jack Ruby was, but to my knowledge, they'd never met. I doubt that Mr. Hunt ever had any private business whatsoever with Jack Ruby. I certainly never saw Ruby at the Hunt offices, and I doubt that Mr. Hunt ever set foot in the Carousel Club.

I went there a number of times, but strictly on business. When we had an important client in from out of town, I would rent him the presidential suite at the Adolphus Hotel in downtown Dallas, and then take him to the Carousel Club. The dancers there were pretty much all call girls, so the client would pick out one that he liked, and take her back to the hotel for a "date." I have no idea whether Ruby got a cut of the money or not, but it wouldn't surprise me a bit if he did. That's just the kind of guy that I believe Jack Ruby was.

Ruby Shooting Oswald, from the Warren Commission Report

There is one curious footnote to the murder of Oswald, however. When Jack Ruby was taken into custody and searched, police found two transcripts of Hunt's *Life Line* radio program in his pocket.

During Ruby's incarceration, Mr. Hunt wanted to keep up with all of his activities – who sent him mail, who Ruby contacted, and who visited him in jail. I received regular reports during that time, and passed those on to Mr. Hunt.

Oddly enough, in the eyes of the law, today Jack Ruby is considered legally innocent of Oswald's murder, even though the killing was broadcast to over a million viewers. Ruby was tried, convicted, and sentenced to death for the killing. His lawyers got the conviction overturned, however, based on a couple of legal issues that were associated with the trial. This completely erased the conviction.

Before he could be re-tried, Ruby developed pneumonia and was admitted to Parkland Hospital in Dallas. In doing some medical tests, doctors realized he had cancer of the liver, lungs, and brain. Within three weeks of his admittance, on January 3, 1967, in an ironic twist to his story, he died in the same hospital where President Kennedy and Oswald had both been taken. The official cause of death was listed as a pulmonary embolism, secondary to bronchogenic carcinoma, which is lung cancer.

But speaking of Ruby and Oswald, the next section concerning Mr. Hunt and Joseph Civello may suggest an answer to the question of why Jack Ruby shot Lee Harvey Oswald.

Mr. Hunt and Joseph Civello

I mentioned that Mr. Hunt wanted to see Joe Civello just before Oswald was killed, and I should probably say a few more words about him.

Joseph Francis Civello started out with his own crime organization in Dallas, the Civello Gang, but he quickly rose through the ranks of the Piranio Crime Family. By 1956, he was head of organized crime's Southern District of the United States.

About a year after he ascended to power, there was an upheaval in the world of the Cosa Nostra in America. Albert Anastasia, the leader of one of the top five crime families of New York, was assassinated. Much like the famous boardroom meeting in the famous movie *The Godfather*, the mob leaders from cities across the country came to Apalachin, New York, to heal any bad blood and to cement Carlo Gambino's immediate succession to Anastasia's position.

There were so many black Cadillacs and Lincolns in the Upstate New York town that it caught the attention of law enforcement and the FBI. Over sixty bosses were arrested and indicted for conspiracy at the Apalachin meeting, including Dallas' own Joseph Civello. At his trial in 1960, he was sentenced to five years in prison, but Houston defense attorney Percy Foreman managed to get the conviction reversed on appeal a year later in 1961.

Even though he was a free man, Civello could not escape the fact that he had brought attention to organized crime activity in Dallas.

Because he was such a powerful man, Mr. Hunt made sure that he had at least a casual relationship with Civello. In fact, we would occasionally stop by to see him at a liquor

115

store that Civello had at the entrance to Love Field, which was there for the sole purpose of laundering mob money. He maintained several businesses for that reason.

In fact, the *Dallas Morning News* once said that Judge Irving R. Kaufman called Civello a "high ranking criminal who cloaked himself with the facade of legitimate business."

On a few occasions, we met Joe Civello at the Admiral's Club at Love Field just to visit and keep up the business relationship between him and Mr. Hunt. Civello was as nice a person as you could want to meet; he didn't drink or smoke, always wore a suit and tie and tipped his hat to the ladies. Somewhere in the folds of his suit, however, he always had two or three guns at the ready, and should the occasion warrant, he was not afraid to use them.

I remember that on different occasions Mr. Hunt would discuss different theories on how someone could protect himself in the event he was associated with or charged with a serious crime. Again, H.L. Hunt believed that the *Life Line* program was effective in having voters expel those from office who needed to be removed, but the process took too much time.

In these vague discussions concerning when a death of a person occurred, Civello would almost always have the same answers, such as: (1) Hire an unknown to do the violent act; (2) then kill the unknown who did the act; (3) if the killer was not killed, then in that case convince him that he could not turn against you; (4) and most important, never let the unknown that you hired ever go to court – *always make him plead guilty.*

116

As far as I know, Mr. Hunt never acted on this advice, but if he had any questions regarding any shady activity, Joseph Civello was the one that he turned to for information.

On another note regarding Mr. Civello, when the House Select Committee on Assassinations was investigating the whole JFK affair in 1976-79, it observed that Jack Ruby's shooting of Lee Harvey Oswald was a primary reason to suspect that organized crime might have had a hand in the presidential assassination.

While investigating Ruby, the Committee observed that he was a "personal acquaintance" of Joseph Civello and that Civello was tied to other crime bosses such as Carlos Marcello of New Orleans.

According to the official report, the Committee noted that "Oswald and Ruby showed a variety of relationships that may have matured into an assassination conspiracy," but that it "was unable firmly to identify the other gunman or the nature and extent" of such a conspiracy that involved organized crime. They were in effect saying that although the Ruby and Civello relationship looked suspicious, they really couldn't prove anything.

Joseph Civello died on January 17, 1970, in a Dallas hospital. At his funeral a few days later, one of the pallbearers was John Brown, who was a sales manager for HLH Products. I had hired him, and he was a key Hunt employee that reported only to me and to Mr. Hunt. I've always wondered about his connection to Mr. Civello, and why a reputed mob boss would have such close ties to the Hunt company.

There is one more story that I remember about Joe Civello, however. In 1962 Mr. Hunt called me into his

117

office and asked me to contact Civello and ask him what Chicago bank his "associates" would recommend. Of course, I knew that Mr. Hunt was talking about organized crime figures in the Windy City.

I contacted Mr. Civello and made the request; a day or so later he called me back and gave me the name of a specific bank: the Continental Illinois National Bank. I relayed that information back to Mr. Hunt, who immediately opened a checking account at that bank with an initial deposit of $250,000... which would be over two million dollars in today's dollars. That was the last time the account was ever mentioned. I have no idea what it was used for, what funds were paid out of it, or to who any payments were made.

To this day it strikes me as rather strange, however. First of all, we had no direct business in Chicago at the time. We didn't have an office there, so it seemed odd to have a checking account in a bank in that city. Believe me, if the company was starting any project in Chicago, not only would I have known about it, but I would have spent time there getting the operation set up. There was simply no need for this act. Mr. Hunt had a Dallas bank, a New York bank and even a Swiss bank. A Chicago bank was completely unnecessary.

The large amount of money that was used to open the account was also puzzling – $250,000.00 was an incredible sum in 1962... over two million dollars today. Who in the world would open a checking account with two million dollars in it? Not only that, however, but at a bank that had been designated by organized crime leaders.

Looking back, however, one of the most interesting things is the timing of the whole thing. Mr. Hunt opened the checking account in 1962, and in the next year John Fitzgerald Kennedy would be dead along with his alleged assassin. I am not saying that there is any correlation at all between these things, but you have to admit that the timing is at least a bit coincidental. We will probably never know what the purpose was for this mysterious checking account.

HUNT OIL COMPANY

DALLAS, TEXAS

W. B. BEEMAN
SECRETARY-TREASURER

July 13, 1962

Mr. Donald M. Graham,
  Vice Chairman of the Board
Continental Illinois National Bank
Chicago, Illinois

Dear Sir:

     We wish to open an account for this Company with you and accordingly enclose our check in the amount of $250,000.00. Will you please furnish us with duplicate deposit slip, your customary form of corporate resolution, and signature cards for specimen signatures of those persons authorized to check on the account.

     As a matter of information, those officers who will be authorized to check on this account are as follows:

               H. L. Hunt, President
               W. B. Beeman, Secretary-Treasurer
               David Schaffnit, Assistant Secretary-Treasurer
               B. M. Shea, Jr., Cashier

          Your assistance in this matter will be appreciated.

                                   Yours very truly,

WBB/pg
Enclosure

bcc: Mr. H. L. Hunt

The letter opening the aforementioned bank account

119

The "Dear Mr. Hunt" Letter

Let me say again that I'm not interested in addressing all of the conspiracy theories surrounding the JFK assassination that involve – or clear – H.L. Hunt. But there has been a lot of discussion and speculation over the years about a letter that Lee Harvey Oswald supposedly wrote to Mr. Hunt, and because that theoretically involves him directly, I thought that I would mention it.

A letter surfaced during the investigation into the Kennedy assassination that simply read:

Nov. 8, 1963
Dear Mr. Hunt,
I would like information concerding [sic] my position.
I am asking only for information. I am suggesting that we discuss the matter fully before any steps are taken by me or anyone else.
Thank you,
Lee Harvey Oswald

This letter showed up in our interoffice mail system after the assassination, and that in and of itself wasn't peculiar. The 1960s were a more innocent age; people will find the stories in this book of getting on an airplane with a briefcase full of money or using an airline ticket in someone else's name to be altogether unbelievable. In reality, the idea of security was nothing even close to what it is today. By the same token, people would often drop off an envelope at the front desk of Hunt Oil, and it would get put into the mail system for delivery to the addressee.

That is exactly how the "Dear Mr. Hunt" letter came in, and since it did, in fact, involve Mr. Hunt, and did, in fact, suggest a meeting with Oswald, we elected to turn it over to the FBI and never saw it again. In private, Mr. Hunt did raise the question as to whether Lee Harvey Oswald could be a *Life Line* listener, something that I think might have been a concern for him.

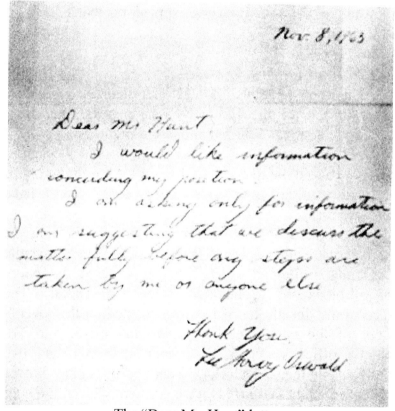

The "Dear Mr. Hunt" letter

This letter has become legendary over the years. Some say it came from an anonymous source, or from

121

Mexico, or from this person or that. It has been said that it was definitely written by Oswald because on one particular curlicue on a letter, or that it couldn't have been written by Oswald because of another particular curlicue on another letter.

Personally, I have no idea whether it was written by Oswald or not. I only know that it showed up in our office and we gave it to the FBI. What they did with it, or how they funneled it to whoever is something that I have no idea about.

Mr. Hunt and Mrs. Oswald

This account begins in 1963 on a Saturday morning a short time after the Kennedy assassination. Mr. Hunt called me at about 6:30 am and asked me to go to work – it wasn't a strange request; we often worked weekends. What he asked me to do when I got there was quite out of the ordinary, however, and to this day I don't have answers for it.

The H.L. Hunt Oil offices were housed in both the Mercantile National Bank Building and the Mercantile Securities Building, which together covered the entire 1800 block of Commerce Street in Dallas. The receptionist for all the offices was located on the seventh floor of the bank building, where my office and Mr. Hunt's office were. A steel door connected the two buildings on the seventh floor. That door was never closed or locked; Hunt employees were constantly using the door to pass between the two adjoining buildings. In fact, only three people had a key to the door: Mr. Hunt had one, an executive with Hunt Oil had another, and I had the third.

That morning Mr. Hunt instructed me to go to the Mercantile Bank Building as soon as possible and lock the steel door on the seventh floor. I was then to check that floor of the Mercantile Bank building to make sure that no Hunt employee was present. Should I encounter anyone, I was to instruct him to go home immediately.

Once that floor was empty, my final assignment was to go down to the lobby and wait there. If any Hunt employees came into work, I was to instruct them to turn around, leave, and not come back that day.

Having completed the first two tasks, I stood in the lobby and waited. There was no activity for a while, until Mr. Hunt came in about 8:30 am. I advised him that all of his security requests had been followed to the letter and that no Hunt employee was in either building.

Mr. Hunt told me that soon a woman would come into the lobby, and I was not to speak to her or even acknowledge her presence. With that, he turned and walked to the elevator and took it upstairs.

A bit later, a woman did, in fact, walk into the building; she was alone and was wearing a modest dress. I recognized her immediately as Marina Oswald, the widow of Lee Harvey Oswald. At that time, her picture was all over the media – newspapers, magazines, and television, and because of the recent events, she was a very recognizable person. There's just no question that it was her.

We didn't speak or even glance at each other; she ignored me and walked directly to the elevator, pushed the button, then disappeared inside. I didn't see what her destination floor was.

I remained in the lobby and had to intercept two Hunt employees who were coming to work. As I'd been told to do, I instructed them to leave immediately and not come back that day.

About twenty minutes, later I heard an elevator door open, and Marina Oswald stepped out. She walked across the lobby and out of the back exit. This was in my line of sight, so I watched as she got into a black automobile with U.S. Government license plates. Once inside, the car drove away.

Not long after that, the elevator opened again, and Mr. Hunt came out. He made no comment whatsoever on what had gone on upstairs, or who he had met with. Instead, he told me to go and unlock the door between the two buildings and take the rest of the day off, which I did.

Looking back, I have no way of knowing what floor Marina visited or what her business was in the bank building that Saturday... but it seems more than a coincidence that Mr. Hunt wanted the offices cleared so that whatever he was doing or whoever he was meeting, it would be completely private. He had never done that before, nor did he ever do it again while I worked

Marina Oswald

for him. At the time, H.L. Hunt's political views were well-known – the Hunt name had been spread throughout

124

the world and many fingers were being pointed at H.L. Hunt involving the death of John F. Kennedy.

I guess it is not surprising that she left the building in a government car; she was under the protection of the Secret Service from the time her husband was arrested until after testifying before the Warren Commission. This would mean, of course, that the government knew of her visit to the bank building that Saturday... and most likely, the truth about what her business there was.

Years later I understand that Marina Oswald, whose married name was Porter by then, was asked whether or not she knew Mr. Hunt, and she firmly stated that she had never met him and had never been to his offices. I guess that it's possible she came to the Mercantile National Bank Building for some other purpose that day, but given Mr. Hunt's strange instructions for security and privacy, and his instruction that a woman would be coming into the lobby, it seems highly unlikely.

But why would she deny meeting with Mr. Hunt? The only people who could answer that question would be Marina, or, when he was alive, Mr. Hunt himself. I suppose it's possible that she didn't know his actual identity that day, or perhaps her life was such a whirlwind after the assassination that she was simply confused as to whom she did or did not meet during that time.

Or, I suppose, it could be that the nature of their discussion itself dictated that they keep the meeting secret.

I have no idea. The one thing that I'm sure of is this: that particular day, in a secured building with no Hunt employees present other than H.L. Hunt himself, and me in the lobby, of course, Marina Oswald entered the building, took an elevator upstairs, and after a short time, departed.

As the years have gone by, I've thought about this incident quite a bit. I could see Mr. Hunt simply wanting to talk to her – he fancied himself an exceptional judge of people, and he genuinely believed that if he could spend ten minutes with anyone he could find the answers to any questions that he had about that person. Mr. Hunt could have used his influence to get some time to talk to Marina just to satisfy his own curiosity.

On the other hand, he could have felt sorry for her. She had been all over the media lamenting the fact that her husband had been accused of killing the president, which alienated her completely. She had no job, no money, two children (Rachel and June) to feed, and she was living with a friend to get by.

I'd seen Mr. Hunt give people money before just to help them out during a difficult time, so I can easily imagine him handing her some cash to help her survive. I remember one occasion when we'd brought a prospective employee over from Hawaii. He worked for Dole Pineapple over there, and we flew him and his family to Dallas, and I got them a hotel in town. Mr. Hunt met with the gentleman and after a few minutes determined that he was not the man for us. He told me to get an airplane ticket back to Hawaii for him and his family, but in addition, instructed me to give him $6,000 cash. Now, I've never heard of anyone being paid so well to fail a job interview, but for some reason, Mr. Hunt wanted to do that. Perhaps he wanted to do something similar for Marina Oswald.

If in fact, Mr. Hunt gave her some money, he probably would have insisted on anonymity, which could be why she never spoke of the meeting. Of course, if that is what happened, then there are many people who might construe that to be something more sinister, like a payoff for one thing or another, but personally, I don't believe that is true.

Some folks would say that it's not surprising that she denies meeting with Mr. Hunt. After all, there were questions about her reliability as a witness that were expressed within the Warren Commission.

There were also contradictions in the things that she said as the years passed; initially, Marina declared that her husband Lee assassinated the president, and later changed that story completely.

Nevertheless, if Mr. Hunt did give her cash, he was not the only one. In his book *The Death of a President*, author William Manchester noted: "Mailbags of checks and cash descended upon Marina, and she led a colorful career. With $70,000 in donations, she engaged a series of business agents. Her husband's Russian diary brought $20,000 and a picture of him holding the Mannlicher-Carcano carbine [the gun used to shoot Kennedy] $5,000. Then she went after the gun itself, arguing that since Oswald was dead it could not be held as evidence. A Denver oilman who wanted it as a souvenir sent her a $10,000 down payment. Marina had spent the money long ago. With affluence, she had acquired mobility. At first, she had told the press that the strongest force in her life was her love for the father of her children; she only wanted to live near his grave. This quickly changed. First, she enrolled at the University of Michigan. Returning to

Dallas, she bought an air-conditioned house, a wardrobe of Neiman-Marcus clothes, and membership in the Music Box, a private club. She became a chain-smoker and a drinker of straight vodka. In the Music Box, she spun through a series of romances. Then, in 1965, in a Texas town called Fate, she became a June bride."

Final thoughts on JFK...

I have always respected those who have a conspiracy theory about the assassination of President John F. Kennedy. Most people just accept or assume the fact that Lee Harvey Oswald pulled the trigger of the 6.5mm Carcano from the sixth floor of the Texas Schoolbook Depository and killed JFK.

After all, Kennedy was dead, Johnson was in office, and life – and business – went on. Looking back, there are some things that I can't explain, such as why Mr. Hunt wanted to know about the conditions around Lee Harvey Oswald in police custody, why he wanted to meet with mob leader Joe Civello, or why he met with Marina Oswald on that very strange Saturday.

Could H.L. Hunt have been following information from an expert and decided that the killing of Oswald would keep questions from being asked and answered?
To be honest, I have no idea. Any such thoughts on my part would be sheer speculation... although it is occasionally interesting to consider.

In 1964 the country was still reeling from the assassination of John Kennedy, and LBJ was looked upon as the savior who had come in after the terrible event and helped heal the country. It was a foregone conclusion that he would be president, but the only question mark was about the vice president.

Many considered Bobby Kennedy to be the frontrunner, but since Bobby and Lyndon Johnson hated each other, that wasn't a viable choice. Looking at alternatives, Johnson believed that Hubert Humphrey could help him in the Midwest and industrial Northeast, so he selected Humphrey as his running mate. To be honest, LBJ could have won the election with either you or I as the V.P., so I never thought that Humphrey helped all that much.

Bobby Kennedy liked Humphrey. Whether that had an effect on it or not, Mr. Hunt thought that Hubert Humphrey was the worst possible choice. But again, it was simply a political move by Johnson to secure a certain block of votes. Between Mr. Hunt and me, we referred to Humphrey as "H.H.H.," meaning "Ha, Ha, Ha."

Hubert H. Humphrey

Still, Lyndon Baines Johnson was the president of the United States of America, and Mr. Hunt could pick up the telephone and call him whenever he wanted, no matter who the vice president was.

With JFK dead and Lyndon in the Oval Office, life – and business – was good.

H.L. Hunt: Motive and Opportunity

130

Part IV: Mr. Hunt and Martin Luther King

I was at Mr. Hunt's Mount Vernon in the summer of 1966 when a reporter from *Playboy* magazine conducted an interview with him. The reporter said, "You have frequently been called a bigot. What's your answer to this charge?"

Mr. Hunt replied, "A bigot is expected to be biased, intolerant, and have a closed mind. Well, I have a consuming curiosity and always like

Dr. Martin Luther King

to hear the different viewpoints. I consider myself open-minded, and therefore not a bigot."

The reporter pressed, "You're not anti-Negro?"

"No," came the answer, "I like the Negroes I have known, and I believe nearly all of them like me."

That blanket statement did not reflect Mr. Hunt's feelings toward one African-American man, however: Dr. Martin Luther King, Jr.

On August 17, 1964, the *New York Times* wrote an article on H.L. Hunt and in it said, "Mr. Hunt and *Life Line* have been accused of being anti-Negro, anti-Jewish, anti-Roman Catholic and anti-union. Mr. Hunt has enjoined *Life Line* from criticizing minority groups or unions. He says he does not believe any of them represent a threat to American society."

In reality, *Life Line* did actively attack individuals, however, and perhaps none more so than Dr. Martin Luther King.

Perceived or real, Dr. King was a serious threat to H.L. Hunt's food companies. On one hand, Hunt's *Life Line* program was carrying on a campaign against King who both Mr. Hunt and J. Edgar Hoover believed to be a Communist; on the other, MLK had the power to call for a boycott against the products that could cripple the Hunt food division.

At the time, HLH Products sold food – a *good deal* of food – into the African-American community. It would not take a lot for King to notice that this company was the main sponsor of *Life Line*, who had been so vehemently attacking him. Calling for a boycott of HLH Products would be a simple and peaceful way for Dr. King to go on the offensive against the *Life Line* radio program's attacks... a fact that Mr. Hunt was well-aware of.

Martin Luther King and J. Edgar Hoover

In that August 1966 interview with *Playboy* magazine, H.L. Hunt was asked whether he regarded Martin Luther King as an "agitator seeking power and votes." Mr. Hunt replied, "I share J. Edgar Hoover's opinion of him."

Playboy further asked, "Are you saying that you agree with Hoover that King is 'the biggest liar in the United States'?" Hunt said, "I cannot detect that King has any regard for the truth, religion, sincerity, peace, morality or the best interest of the Negro people."

I know for a fact that both Hoover and Mr. Hunt believed that King was a dyed-in-the-wool communist, that he was being supported by communists, and that his funds were coming directly from the Communist Party.

Hoover had approached Attorney General Bobby Kennedy to allow the FBI to wiretap King to try to obtain proof of his ties to communism. The Attorney General gave written approval for only limited wiretapping of King's phones for a short period, but Hoover took the liberty of extending the order for his men to look for evidence in any areas of King's life that they wanted.

On November 21, 1964, a letter was sent to King's wife, Coretta, which outlined alleged sexual indiscretions by her husband. A copy of the letter was sent to Dr. King as well, and he not only believed that it came directly from the FBI, but he understood it to be a suggestion that he take his own life. According to the *New York Times* magazine, a copy of the letter is known to exist in J. Edgar Hoover's confidential files at the National Archives.

On Mr. Hunt's part, he brought the full guns of *Life Line* to bear on Martin Luther King – he was probably the subject of more *Life Line* programs than anyone else in the program's history. But while Mr. Hunt felt like he was doing his duty by exposing what he considered to be a true Communist, he was also worried about the damage that King could do to his business.

Dr. King and the Boycott Threat

As previously stated, the Hunt food division, which was the only sponsor of *Life Line*, catered largely to the African-American community with its sales. Mr. Hunt knew that if Martin Luther King decided to retaliate against *Life Line* by calling for a boycott among his loyal followers, it could literally cost him millions of dollars.

After all, Dr. King had led the successful Montgomery Bus Boycott a decade earlier, targeting the Montgomery Bus Line in Alabama. At that time, the ten front seats on a Montgomery bus were reserved for white riders, the ten back seats were designated for black riders, and the fourteen seats in the middle could be used by either, although it was against the law for a black rider and a white rider to sit next to each other. The buses filled from the front to back for whites, and back to front for blacks. Black riders were required to stand and give up their seats to white riders should the need arise.

One fateful day, December 1, 1955, an African-American woman named Rosa Parks was sitting in the middle section. The bus stopped and a white man boarded, and the bus driver ordered everyone in her row to move back. Ms. Parks would not comply and was arrested. She was fined $10 for her violation, along with $4 court cost.

Dr. Martin Luther King met with a group of people at the Mt. Zion Church to discuss a boycott, which although hard-fought, was so successful in the end, that it nearly crippled the bus company financially and eventually led to the end of segregation on the buses.

Several years later, Dr. King participated in the famous March on Washington for Jobs and Freedom that took place on August 28, 1963. Up to 300,000 attended the event, with an estimated 75-80% of whom were African-American. It was one of the largest political rallies for human rights in United States history.

Rosa Parks being fingerprinted after her arrest

At the rally, Dr. King stood up before the Lincoln Memorial and delivered his famous "I have a dream" speech, which included the famous words, "I have a dream that my four little children will one day live in a nation where they will not be judged by the color of their skin but by the content of their character."

This speech cemented King's reputation not only as a gifted orator but an inspirational and motivational force to his followers. Mr. Hunt knew that should King ever call for a boycott of Hunt food products, it would be a devastating blow to the company.

And it wasn't an unrealistic threat. Not only was Mr. Hunt bombarding the public with anti-King messages, but his Hunt food companies had been accused of providing substandard food that was sold in the African-American community.

One thing was certain – as long as Dr. King was continuing to grow in popularity, the Hunt food division was in jeopardy.

Assassination Day

On March 29, 1968, Dr. Martin Luther King, Jr. went to Memphis, Tennessee, in support of the black workers there. A few days later, on April 3, King addressed a rally and delivered his last speech, which included the famous closing:

"And then I got into Memphis. And some began to say the threats, or talk about the threats that were out. What would happen to me from some of our sick white brothers?

"Well, I don't know what will happen now. We've got some difficult days ahead. But it really doesn't matter with me now, because I've been to the mountaintop.

"And I don't mind.

"Like anybody, I would like to live a long life. Longevity has its place. But I'm not concerned about that now. I just want to do God's will. And He's allowed me to go up to the mountain. And I've looked over. And I've seen the Promised Land. I may not get there with you. But I want you to know tonight, that we, as a people, will get to the Promised Land!

"And so I'm happy, tonight.

"I'm not worried about anything.

"I'm not fearing any man!

"Mine eyes have seen the glory of the coming of the Lord!"

The Assassination Scene, Lorraine Motel, Memphis
(Carol M. Highsmith, photographer, Library of Congress)

Dr. King was booked into his usual room at the Lorraine Motel, room 306. The next evening he walked out into the night air in front of the room. At 6:01 pm, April 4, 1968, as he stood on the motel's second-floor balcony, a rifle shot rang through the air. The bullet hit Dr. King, entered through his right cheek, smashed his jaw, and then traveled down his spinal cord before lodging in his shoulder.

He was rushed to St. Joseph's Hospital and after emergency surgery, Dr. King died at 7:05 pm.

Right after the shot was fired, people saw a man who was later identified as James Earl Ray running from a boarding house across the street from the motel. A rifle and binoculars were both found there with Ray's fingerprints.

Mr. Hunt received a phone call within minutes after the assassination from J. Edgar Hoover and was told about the death of Dr. King.

Mr. Hunt Hits the Road

On the evening of the assassination, Mr. Hunt called me and gave me two things to do immediately. The first was to cancel any *Life Line* programs that were anti-King, and the other was to get him and his wife out of Dallas right away.

He had been receiving many threatening phone calls at his house – much more than he had after JFK's assassination – and he was concerned. His Mount Vernon home had no real security, no fence, and his name was listed in the phone book just like everyone else's. Along with the phone calls, a few cars had pulled into the driveway and fired shots at the house. Mr. Hunt had absolutely no protection at the house – you could drive right up to it; there were no guards (armed or otherwise), and to my knowledge, Mr. Hunt didn't own a gun. In fact, in case someone came up to the house that he wanted to scare away, I kept him supplied with a supply of "Baby Giant Firecrackers." He would simply light one and throw it out a window. That was the extent of his security measures. Mr. Hunt was justifiably afraid, so he asked me where he could go so as not to be easily recognized.

I suggested the Holiday Inn in El Paso. I had been a guest there just a few days earlier; it was a new motel and I don't think that Mr. Hunt had ever spent any time in El Paso. I called and reserved a room in my own name, and then drove out to the airport and bought two tickets to El Paso – one in the name of "John Curington," and the other in the name of "M.A. Curington." After that, I went to Mount Vernon and picked up H.L. and Ruth Hunt, gave them their airline tickets, and took them to the Love Field Airport. In those days you didn't have to show any identification to get on a plane, so I knew that wouldn't be a problem.

I went back to the office, and just like I had done after JFK's death, I assembled a team of Hunt Oil secretaries and had them call the *Life Line* radio stations and advise them not to air any of the programs involving Martin Luther King.

On Monday morning after the Friday assassination of Dr. King, J. Edgar Hoover called the office to speak to Mr. Hunt. When he was told that he was unavailable, Hoover asked to speak to "John," which was the only name that he knew me by.

Mr. Hoover wanted to know the whereabouts of Mr. Hunt and asked me if I knew how to get hold of him. I explained that he was in El Paso, and would probably be there a few days – or at least until the news coverage of the death of Martin Luther King died down. Hoover asked me to call Mr. Hunt and have him come to Washington immediately. I assured him that I would relay the message as soon as we hung up.

I called El Paso and got Mr. Hunt on the phone, and then advised him of Hoover's request. He said that he wanted to leave for Washington just as soon as I could get the airline tickets arranged and reservations at the Mayflower Hotel.

After doing so, I called Mr. Hoover back and told him that Mr. Hunt would soon be on his way. I gave him the flight number and time of arrival, knowing that Hoover would make the rest of the arrangements on his end.

Mr. Hunt didn't get back to Dallas for several days, and when he did, he didn't say anything about the call from Hoover or the trip to Washington. It was simply business as usual.

When Mr. Hunt checked out of the Holiday Inn in El Paso, he instructed the hotel to send the room bill to John Curington at the Hunt Oil Company's Dallas address. Again, this was not at all strange or out of character. What was unusual was that Mr. Hunt called me from Washington and told me that the hotel bill was being sent to me, and I was not to pay it with a Hunt Oil Company check – instead I was to obtain a cashier's check in my name and mail it directly to El Paso. He did not want the name H.L. Hunt disclosed or associated with it in any way.

I have no idea why J. Edgar Hoover wanted to meet with Mr. Hunt, but clearly, it was very important to the FBI Director.

Mr. Hunt and Percy Foreman

When King was shot, witnesses saw a man who was later identified as James Earl Ray fleeing from a house across the street from the motel where he had been renting a room. A rifle and binoculars were found nearby that had Ray's fingerprints.

Two months after Martin Luther King was killed, Ray was arrested at London Heathrow Airport, attempting to leave the United Kingdom on a Canadian passport.

I know that Mr. Hunt had a number of conversations with Hoover after the arrest and extradition. Hoover was adamant that the murder of Martin Luther King be placed squarely on the shoulders of James Earl Ray.

This was a concern because H.L. Hunt lived in fear that if Ray did go to trial he could have testified that messages that he got from the *Life Line* radio program could have influenced him to shoot Martin Luther King. If this had come out, Mr. Hunt believed that he personally could have been indicted.

I sometimes think back to one of the things that Joe Civello had told Mr. Hunt – that if you had someone killed, you must never let the unknown that you hired ever go to court – *always make him plead guilty*. And of course, when I consider Lee Harvey Oswald, I can't help but recall another piece of advice from Civello: hire an unknown to do the violent act and then kill the unknown who did the act.

When James Earl Ray began to have a falling out with his attorney, Texas trial lawyer Percy Foreman flew to Memphis and showed up at the Shelby County Jail. There he convinced Ray to fire his original attorney and hire him.

One day I was in Mr. Hunt's office, and he called Percy Foreman with me sitting there. He told Foreman that he had a young attorney – meaning me – who had some very interesting ideas on who killed King.

Percy Foreman replied that he'd be happy to talk to this fellow and to have him stop by his office.

At Mr. Hunt's instruction, I traveled to call on Percy Foreman with a briefcase and laid it on the desk in front of him. "I have one hundred and twenty-five thousand reasons why James Earl Ray should plead guilty to killing Martin Luther King," I said.

Foreman looked at me and said, "Well, just leave them with me, and I'll take a look at them." I walked out of the room, not having been there more than a minute or two.

I left the $125,000, which would be just under a million dollars in today's money, and sure enough, James Earl Ray entered a guilty plea.

Three days later, Ray asked the judge for a change of plea, a new attorney, and a trial by jury. His request was denied.

When the *Los Angeles Times* newspaper eulogized Percy Foreman on his death on August 26, 1988, it included the notation, "He persuaded James Earl Ray to plead guilty to the 1968 slaying of King, the Nobel Prize-winning civil rights leader, in exchange for a 99-year sentence. Ray charged later that Foreman pressured him into the plea by saying that the odds were 99% certain he would go to the electric chair if he faced a jury in Tennessee. Ray contended that he only purchased the rifle used in the Memphis assassination and gave it to a man named Raoul.

He charged that Foreman failed to investigate two mysterious Louisiana men who, he contended, would have helped his case."

James Earl Ray denied killing King until he died in prison from complications of hepatitis C. According to records at the King Center, the King family has come to believe that James Earl Ray had nothing to do with the assassination of Dr. Martin Luther King.

Percy Foreman continued to be tied to Mr. Hunt, his family, and his associates… including many of the names that have appeared in this book.

Final Thoughts on MLK…

I paid $125,000 to Percy Foreman on Mr. Hunt's behalf to get James Earl Ray to confess to the killing of Martin Luther King. Although that is exactly what happened, Ray soon recanted his confession, and to this day the King family believes that he was innocent of the murder.

Why was it so important for Mr. Hunt to have a confession from Ray? And if Ray was indeed guilty, why did his attorney require such a substantial, under-the-table payment?

There's something else that has always weighed on my mind. That phone conversation that I was privy to between Mr. Hunt and Percy Foreman was very short and to the point, and the promise of money was just a veiled, casual thing. My own conversation with Foreman wasn't much more. Surely some prior groundwork had been done, and I have to wonder if it hadn't been done between J. Edgar Hoover, Mr. Hunt, and Percy Foreman.

Unfortunately, the answers to all those things and many other questions died with Mr. Hunt.

Part V: Mr. Hunt and Bobby Kennedy

The assassination of John F. Kennedy made the country grieve and lifted the beloved former president almost to the status of sainthood. The state funeral, complete with John Jr. saluting his fallen father, cemented JFK's place in history and in the hearts of the nation.

A few years later, the country's wave of emotion

Robert "Bobby" Kennedy

was apparently going to wash over onto Robert Francis "Bobby" Kennedy – something that deeply worried H.L. Hunt.

Bobby Kennedy, LBJ, and Bobby Baker

Robert Gene "Bobby" Baker first met Lyndon Johnson when LBJ was elected to the Senate in 1948. Even as a young man, Baker was active in the political world. He started out as a Senate page and worked his way up to the position of Senate secretary to the majority Leader. He ingratiated himself to all the important congressmen, and became a Washington "insider."

When LBJ met Bobby Baker, he was told that he "knew where all the bodies were buried," so Johnson embraced the young man as his friend, confidant, and adviser.

Baker was one of the founders of the Quorum Club, a private organization housed adjacent to a Senate office building that was said to be a place for congressmen and other prominent figures to dine, enjoy drinks, and hook up with women to entertain them. One of these congressmen was allegedly a Senator named John Fitzgerald Kennedy.

In 1962 while LBJ was vice president, Baker and a friend, Fred Black, set up a corporation named Serv-U that provided vending machines for programs and organizations that were established under federal grants. It was rumored that as part of the normal operation of the corporation, bribery and sexual favors were used as influence with congressmen.

Robert Kennedy – now the attorney general – began to look even more carefully at Bobby Baker. He uncovered the fact that Baker had ties to many influential men, ranging from Texas oil millionaires to Mafia chieftains. Because of the ties between Baker and LBJ, the trail soon led to Lyndon Johnson and included even more shady deals, such as the awarding of a $7 billion contract for a fighter plane to Texas company General Dynamics.

A special Senate investigation was launched against both Baker and Johnson, and it seemed as if it was going to bury them both. Baker resigned from his positions in October 1963, a month before JFK was assassinated. Lyndon Johnson was still under investigation, but that was dropped when he became president in November.

This destroyed Bobby Kennedy's plans to have LBJ not only dropped from the 1964 presidential ticket but indicted for criminal activity as well. John F. Kennedy's death enraged brother Bobby, not just because of the loss that he felt, but also because it catapulted LBJ into his brother's chair in the Oval Office. It also wasn't lost on Bobby that his brother had been killed in LBJ's home state, on a political visit that Johnson had encouraged.

Bobby and the 1968 Election

During LBJ's first full term as president, Mr. Hunt called him at the White House and said something to the effect of, "Lyndon, you've had a good go at this, but I don't think that you should run next time around." Mr. Hunt was very, very good at reading a situation, and I believe that he saw the divisions in the Democratic party, and the mounting tension over the Vietnam War, and knew that Johnson wasn't going to be able to win.

Most political analysts believe that Johnson withdrew from the race once Bobby Kennedy announced his intention to run, but it was much more than that. LBJ knew that Mr. Hunt's support – both financial and political – had been one of the cornerstones of his success, and that had disappeared.

By 1968, it was clear that Bobby Kennedy was going to get the nomination and probably win the presidency. This was a serious concern for Mr. Hunt because, in his opinion, Bobby would be ten times worse than JFK ever was. Mr. Hunt felt that Jack was kind of lazy and a do-nothing sort of fellow, but Bobby was very aggressive.

Bobby Kennedy hated Lyndon Johnson and knew that Mr. Hunt had depended on LBJ for a number of things on his personal agenda. Mr. Hunt was concerned that RFK would be strong enough and vengeful enough to hurt him in any possible way. Mr. Hunt was in the most vulnerable position of his entire business life.

The California Trip

In the late spring of 1968, Mr. Hunt came in and told me that he wanted to go to Los Angeles the next day. I was to get tickets for both of us, along with a room at the Ambassador Hotel in Los Angeles... even though we had never stayed at the Ambassador before. Our usual accommodations were at the Beverly Hills Hotel.

The trip itself wasn't an unusual request, however, because we went to California every month or so. I made the arrangements, and when we arrived, Mr. Hunt told me two things. First, he asked me to contact Wendell Niles. This was a man whose father was Bob Hope's TV announcer, so Wendell was very well connected in L.A. We had him on the payroll so that he would keep us advised as to what was going on in the movie industry and in the Los Angeles area. Mr. Hunt wanted me to find out from Niles exactly what Bobby Kennedy had been doing in California, including where he'd been, where he was going, and who was in his inner circle. I left Wendell a message to call me at the Hotel.

We arrived at the Ambassador Hotel, and Mr. Hunt told me that he was going to have a private meeting with a fellow, and for me to just go to my room and wait to hear from Wendell. It was clear that whatever the business might be, I wasn't going to be privy to it. This was a little unusual. I contacted Wendell Niles while Mr. Hunt had dinner with the mystery person, and afterward never commented on it.

The Ambassador Hotel on Wilshire Blvd in L.A.

I don't know who it was or what they discussed. When I saw Mr. Hunt later, I gave him the information that Wendell Niles had provided. We left to return to Dallas the next day with nothing being said about the business in L.A. – Mr. Hunt never even hinted as to why we made the trip.

Within two weeks, Robert F. Kennedy would be dead.

Assassination Day

On June 5, 1968, Kennedy had recently won the California primary election, and on that night, he had just finished addressing his campaign supports in the ballroom

149

of the Ambassador Hotel in Los Angeles. It was just after midnight. His only security was a former FBI agent and two former professional athletes.

Kennedy was planning on simply walking through the ballroom on his way to a gathering elsewhere in the hotel, but campaign aide Fred Dutton diverted him through the hotel's kitchen for a quick, impromptu press conference. As he followed the hotel's maître d' through a narrow kitchen hallway, he reached out to shake a busboy's hand, and Sirhan Sirhan moved over to him and repeatedly fired a .22 caliber Iver-Johnson Cadet revolver.

Robert F. Kennedy was rushed to the Central Receiving Hospital, where doctors performed heart massage and stabilized his heartbeat. He was then transferred a few blocks away to the Hospital of the Good Samaritan for surgery to have the bullets removed and wounds treated.

In spite of the extensive neurosurgery, he died at 1:44 am, twenty-six hours after the shooting.

Kennedy had been hit three times. One bullet entered his head behind his right ear, sending fragments into his brain. The other two bullets entered at the rear of his right armpit; one exited from his chest and the other lodged in the back of his neck.

I personally found out about the shooting about five minutes after it happened. My phone rang, and it was Wendell Niles from L.A. with the news. I hung up and immediately called Mr. Hunt, who didn't express any interest one way or the other. He said something like, "Okay, we'll talk about that tomorrow," and that was the extent of it.

Sirhan Bishara Sirhan

Unlike the killing of John F. Kennedy, where Oswald's role of assassin has been repeatedly challenged, the murder of Bobby Kennedy was up close and personal, and in front of a room full of witnesses.

When the shots were fired, author George Plimpton, author Pete Hamill, football star and Hall of Famer Rosey Grier, and 1960 Olympic gold medalist Rafer Johnson struggled with Sirhan Sirhan to subdue him.

Four days later, on June 9, Sirhan Bishara Sirhan confessed to the police that he had murdered Bobby Kennedy. The confession was not allowed in court, however, and he was put on trial and given the death sentence. This was later commuted down to life imprisonment.

Sirhan Sirhan

In what seems like a straightforward case, there are actually a number of different conspiracy theories surrounding the assassination. One is that another shooter fired the fatal shot, which is a possibility that is supported by the chief medical examiner-coroner for the County of Los Angeles who said that the fatal shot was behind Kennedy's right ear, and had been fired at a distance of approximately one inch, something that Sirhan Sirhan could not have done.

Another theory is that Sirhan Sirhan was psychologically programmed and controlled by someone else, a theory that is supported by psychologist and hypnosis expert Dr. Eduard Simson-Kallas after many hours of work with Sirhan Sirhan in 1969 after his conviction. This is widely referred to as the "Manchurian Candidate" theory, named after the famous 1962 movie starring Frank Sinatra.

Whether or not he acted alone will probably never be known for sure, but one thing is certain: Sirhan Bishara Sirhan claimed after his incarceration, and ever since, to have absolutely no memory of the assassination of Bobby Kennedy.

As this book was being finalized, two very interesting things happened. First of all, Robert F. Kennedy, Jr., went public with the story that he had examined the autopsy of his father, and even met with Sirhan Sirhan, and did not believe that he fired the fatal shot. RFK Jr. is now calling for a new investigation of the death of his father.

At about the same time another someone else made a similar demand: Paul Schrade, a union official and friend to Robert Kennedy. Mr. Schrade was walking through the pantry of the Ambassador Hotel with Kennedy that night, and he was shot in the forehead when RFK was gunned down. He survived, and all these years later, believes that Sirhan Sirhan was not the only shooter.

The Money Delivery

Approximately four to six weeks after the assassination, Mr. Hunt called me in and told me that he needed to send $40,000 to California to a fellow, but he didn't want me to take it. Instead, he told me to pick somebody in the organization that I trusted but who wouldn't be readily connectable to the Hunt company.

That was a lot of money – keep in mind that in today's world, that would be almost $300,000.

I selected a man named Mark Deering, who was in a different building from ours. He came over to the First National Bank Building, and Mr. Hunt personally gave him two envelopes with the money – each had $20,000. Mr. Hunt didn't give him any instructions; he just gave him the cash. I told Mark that a man named Tom would meet him at the airport, and he would give the money to him. Remember that at that time, no one searched bags before the flight, not even a carry-on, so it was a trivial task to take two envelopes full of money onto a plane and fly across the country.

When Mark landed in L.A., another man – not Tom – was at the airport to collect the money. Since it wasn't the fellow that we were expecting, Mark phoned me for further instructions, and I informed him we weren't going to release the money to anyone but Tom.

Mark relayed this to the man, who called his boss to explain the situation. The fellow who was supposed to be the recipient of the money – Tom – finally spoke to Mark, and told him that they would meet at the Ambassador Hotel for the handoff, which they did. It is curious that they met at the location where Robert Kennedy was assassinated.

Mark returned to Dallas and told me that he had delivered the money as ordered. He turned in a handwritten report to me, and that was the last thing that I ever heard about it. I have no idea what the money was for, or why it had to be delivered by someone who wasn't that identifiable with the Hunt organization. I still have his report, which follows:

153

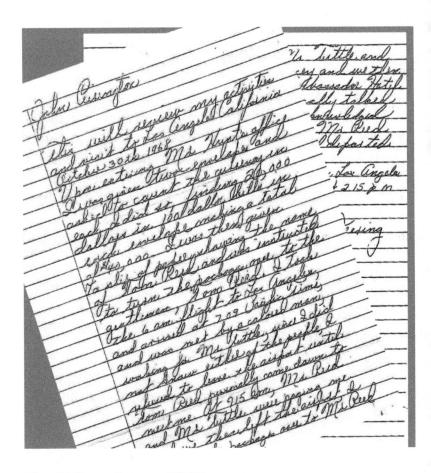

Final Thoughts on RFK...

The strangest thing about our California trip was that I'd been left out of whatever business meeting that Mr. Hunt had. I'd delivered large sums of money to pay off his gambling debts in the past and also collected from the people that owed him. I'd been a part of every aspect of his business, so I cannot imagine what transpired that night.

And then there's the payment that had to be delivered after RFK was killed – along with the fact that it had to be delivered by someone besides me. On most every occasion, I was the only one that Mr. Hunt would trust with a cache of money like that.

All of these facts are ingredients interesting, and although at the time I knew better than to even ponder what had gone on, at this point in my life, I have to look back with more than a little curiosity, and a few questions:

- Why did we make such a sudden trip to Los Angeles?
- Why did we stay at the Ambassador Hotel, a place that we had never used before?
- Who did Mr. Hunt meet alone?
- Why was Wendell Niles instructed to give daily reports regarding Robert Kennedy?
- Why did H.L. Hunt show no interest when I told him within a few minutes of Robert Kennedy's shooting?
- Why did the $40,000 payoff end up at the Ambassador Hotel?

I don't have the answers to these questions, but they are very interesting to think about. I do know for a fact that Mr. Hunt believed that Bobby Kennedy would get the 1968 Democratic nomination and that after he would be elected president of the United States – something that was almost unthinkable to H.L. Hunt.

Part VI: Mr. Hunt and Jimmy Hoffa

Jimmy Hoffa was a union activist as a young man and quickly rose through the ranks of the International Brotherhood of Teamsters. He also became involved in organized crime in parallel to his union activities and was indicted and convicted on any number of charges related to that in 1964.

James "Jimmy" Hoffa

For a man such as H.L. Hunt, who had thousands of non-union employees, a man like Hoffa represented a serious threat.

Mr. Hunt and Mr. Hoffa

In the 1960s two of the most powerful men in the world were: 1) H.L. Hunt, the world's richest man with widespread business interests, and 2) James Riddle "Jimmy" Hoffa, the world's most powerful labor union organizer. Each had a very powerful and personal motive for everything that they did.

H.L. Hunt did not want any of his employees, who numbered in the thousands, to be involved in a labor union in any form, shape or fashion.

Jimmy Hoffa, on the other hand, believed that every employee in the nation should be a member of a union and pay monthly dues.

Mr. Hunt was very proud of his working relationship with his employees. They were paid fair wages, respected in their job duties, and afforded many other benefits. It was his belief that by providing above average attention to each and every employee, it would not only benefit the company but would benefit the employee as well.

Jimmy Hoffa believed that if an employee became a union member that not only would the union benefit, but the employee would get better working conditions.

Each side had strong talking points, and each side had something to gain.

In addition to many, many business ventures, H.L. Hunt was involved in opening several food-processing plants throughout the United States. The plants employed a good many people, which caught the attention of the unions.

Whenever a union organizer would visit the city where one of the plants was located, Mr. Hunt would send me there. I made contact with one or two of the most prominent men in that town – men who shared the same views as Mr. Hunt as far as labor unions. I would solicit their help in getting the union organizer out of the town.

Normally, the best approach would be to work with the chief of police, who would, in turn, find ways to compromise the organizer and force him to leave town. He would watch the organizer closely – for example, looking for any possible violation that might result in an arrest.

In one instance, the union organizer had a goal of getting into the oil well drilling companies. There were many employees in most drilling companies and higher wages were paid. This union organizer case took place in Louisiana, and in the course of trying to keep him out of the oil business, the organizer was killed. An attorney was making an attempt to get a wrongful death suit filed over the union organizer's death. H.L. Hunt was most concerned that he could have been named in such a suit, because the man who did the killing was soon hired as a Louisiana police officer, and the murder of the union organizer was swept under the rug. I don't think that Mr. Hunt wanted the organizer killed, he just wanted him to leave his drilling operations alone.

From month to month and day to day, the union became more aggressive in its efforts to organize the various business ventures of Mr. Hunt.

Jimmy Hoffa and Bobby Kennedy

Jimmy Hoffa was a ninth-grade dropout who started out his career as a grocery worker, where he was subjected to low pay, long hours, and terrible conditions. He stood up to the boss and gained the respect of the other workers. When he finally left the job, he had been noticed by the union and was offered the job as organizer with the Local 299 of the Teamsters in Detroit in 1932.

By 1933 the Teamsters had 75,000 members, but by 1936 – in some part due to Hoffa – the membership had more than doubled and grown to 170,000 members.

Jimmy Hoffa rose through the ranks as the union grew; 420,000 by 1939, and over a million members by 1951.

In 1952, he was appointed to be the vice president of the Teamsters and assumed the role of president in 1957 when the former union president was indicted and convicted of fraud. Hoffa had become a very powerful man, and he was forced to do business with many members of organized crime families. Some say that he had become little more than a gangster himself, although on a grand scale – he basically controlled all of the over-the-road truckers in America.

In 1957 he was faced with his first major criminal investigation, although he managed to escape conviction. There were some storm clouds looming on the horizon, however, in the embodiment of Robert Francis "Bobby" Kennedy.

Bobby Kennedy had been the chief counsel for the McClellan Senate Labor Subcommittee who first went after Hoffa in 1957 and was frustrated by the inability to bring him down. When JFK was elected president, he appointed Bobby as the U.S. attorney general – and Bobby immediately launched the biggest crusade against organized crime that the country had ever seen... and this included Jimmy Hoffa.

In fact, Bobby Kennedy put together his own special "Get Hoffa" squad within the Justice Department. They reportedly engaged in activities that were questionably legal to try to bring down the head of the Teamsters.

The Kennedy brothers hated Jimmy Hoffa, and Jimmy Hoffa hated them right back with an equal ferocity. When JFK was assassinated, Hoffa reportedly stood up on the chair in the restaurant where he was dining and cheered, adding, "I hope the worms eat his eyes!"

Bobby Kennedy must have felt victorious when Hoffa was convicted in 1964 of attempted bribery of a grand juror, a crime for which he was sentenced to eight years. Later that year, he was convicted of fraud for improper use of the Teamsters' pension fund. For that, he received a five-year prison term that was set to be served concurrently.

Following his incarceration, Robert F. Kennedy resigned as attorney general to run for the U.S. Senate position from New York, which he won.

Jimmy Hoffa in – and out of – Prison

Jimmy Hoffa served time in the Federal Bureau of Prisons from the two 1964 convictions. Being incarcerated did slow Hoffa down personally, but it did not stop the unions from continuing their efforts to organize workers.

H.L. Hunt, as usual, had powerful friends in Washington and was very close to a United States senator who had the reputation of being able to work with Hoffa. Mr. Hunt came up with a plan where he would use his influence and political contacts to get Jimmy Hoffa released from prison, and then arrange a pardon from him from the president himself, Richard Nixon.

During the period of time that this deal was being made, it was obvious that there would have to be some payoffs and such. A sum of $125,000 in cash was going to be required, and of course, that money would have to come from Mr. Hunt.

There was an attorney out of Washington who was Jimmy Hoffa's man, and he was to pick up the money; his name was Sidney Zachary.

Zachery had been in H.L. Hunt's office on two other occasions that I recall. On the day that the $125,000 was paid, I met him with the money in a briefcase at the Cabana Motor Hotel, which was built and owned by the Teamsters Union on I-35 (Stemmons Freeway) in Dallas. Entertainer Doris Day also owned a piece of the hotel.

Postcard from the Cabana Motor Hotel

It's quite a coincidence that in 1985, the Cabana, which had once welcomed the Beatles, Led Zeppelin, and Jimi Hendrix, became a correctional facility – a jail. According to the FBI, back in 1963, Jack Ruby was seen at the Bon Vivant Room of the Dallas Cabana about midnight before President Kennedy was assassinated. Today, it is just around the corner from the Margaret Hunt

Hill Bridge, which was named for H.L. Hunt's oldest daughter because of her position in Dallas as an heiress and philanthropist. This is just a note of interest in how things come back around and connect.

At the time when I met Zachery at the Cabana, it was simply a hotel with a popular nightspot. I gave him the briefcase with the $125,000, and he did not open it. There were no papers signed; we simply shook hands, and I left the Cabana.

This Hoffa attorney, Sidney Zachery, left Dallas and was to fly to Atlanta, Georgia. I later got word that this man had gone out to dinner that night in Atlanta, and while he was dining, the restaurant caught on fire. The one person killed in the incident was Sidney. I have never had any proof of that and have never heard any more information whatsoever.

If in fact Sidney was killed, I have to wonder what happened to the money. Had he already delivered it to someone? I don't know the answer to those questions – I can honestly say that I'd handed this man a briefcase with $125,000 in it without knowing where it was going or what it was for.

What I do know is that H.L. Hunt had made a deal with Jimmy Hoffa. The agreement was that Hunt would arrange for Hoffa to be released from prison and then given a presidential pardon, and Jimmy Hoffa would pledge that no union organizers would ever enter a Hunt business. This arrangement cost $125,000, and in the end, it was probably worth it for Mr. Hunt. I have no idea how this money was spread around; after all, it would be the equivalent of well over half a million dollars in today's world.

163

Interesting enough, the Teamsters threw their support to Nixon in the 1972 election, something that raised more than a few eyebrows. I can't help but wonder if this was part of the deal as well. However, that wasn't the end of the money trail.

Periodically, additional payments were necessary, and a Louisiana Government Official was used to pass the money on to Hoffa and his Teamsters, which in turn kept unionization out of the Hunt companies. In fact, Jimmy Hoffa personally pulled a union organizer out of a Hunt company in Muncie, Indiana. With the Hunt/Hoffa deal, and the continued payouts, the Teamsters used strong-arm tactics to keep any union issues out of Hunt operations.

Assassination Day

On July 30, 1975, Jimmy Hoffa went to the Machus Red Fox Restaurant just outside of Detroit at about 2:00 in the afternoon. He was supposedly going to meet two other Mafia leaders: Anthony Giacalone and Anthony Provenzano. He arrived in the parking lot first and waited for about thirty minutes before calling his wife to tell her that he suspected that he'd been stood up by his associates. He told her that he was going to wait a few minutes longer before giving up. That would be the last time that his wife ever spoke to him – she was the one that first reported him missing that evening.

About 2:45 pm, Hoffa was seen getting into a car in the restaurant parking lot with a number of other men. It was the last time that anyone saw Jimmy Hoffa alive.

His car was found at the restaurant, unlocked, but with no clues as to what might have happened to him. Anthony Giacalone and Anthony Provenzano both denied having scheduled a meeting with Hoffa and produced alibis. The authorities ruled that they were not near the restaurant that afternoon.

James Riddle "Jimmy" Hoffa was declared legally dead on July 30, 1982, seven years after he pulled into the parking lot of the Machus Red Fox Restaurant.

Personally, I was told that he was shot, and then his body was put through an industrial meat grinder – clothes, shoes, belt, watch and all. Whatever was left would be very easy to dispose of, which is probably the reason that no one has ever found his body.

Of course, there are stories that his body was buried in the concrete of Giants Stadium, or in some highway or a dozen other places. I believe that the killers would never take a chance to have the body found, so if it wasn't disposed of as I was told, then it was most certainly completely destroyed in some other fashion – cremation, possibly.

Final Thoughts on Hoffa...

Mr. Hunt passed away approximately eight months before Jimmy Hoffa was killed, but he was still indirectly tied to his death. Unlike the cases of Robert F. Kennedy, Martin Luther King, and Bobby Kennedy, no one was ever arrested – or even officially accused – of the murder of Jimmy Hoffa, and Mr. Hunt had no influence on that person or persons.

What Mr. Hunt did do, however, was to set the wheels in motion that allowed the murder to occur. He made the offer to get Hoffa out of prison to protect his own business – to prevent the unionization of his companies.

165

I doubt if Hoffa would have ever been touched in prison; he probably would have served his time, and then have been released to find that the union had moved on without him. Instead, Mr. Hunt arranged for his release and altered the course of his life forever.

Upon his release, the Teamsters paid Hoffa a lump-sum retirement of $1.7 million, which was unheard of at that time. As part of his release, however, Jimmy Hoffa was forbidden to participate in any union activities until March 1980, yet he still had some degree of influence, and he honored the agreement set up by Mr. Hunt. Not only that, but the new administration of the unions honored this agreement as well.

I would think that this falls under the category of "honor among thieves." Even though the unions didn't technically have to honor the agreement that Hoffa made with Mr. Hunt, they did.

Jimmy Hoffa couldn't leave well enough alone, however, and instead of enjoying his life as a wealthy man, he went to court to fight the "no union activity" part of his pardon... and lost. Nevertheless, he still began working on his power base in the organization, and many believe that is why he was killed.

Mr. Hunt had passed away by then, and therefore had no connection to the murder... other than arranging for Hoffa's release, which started the ball rolling on the whole tragic affair.

Part VII: The Accused

Jimmy Hoffa's killers were never found, and Mr. Hunt's influence in that incident was much different from his possible connections with the other three assassinations. In those other three cases, there was a specific person who was accused, if not tried and convicted, of each murder: Lee Harvey Oswald for John F. Kennedy, James Earl Ray for Martin Luther King, and Sirhan Sirhan for Bobby Kennedy.

Oswald   Ray   Sirhan

There are similarities that exist between these three accused assassins that are worth taking a little closer look at – specifically, the various aspects of their individual lives before they became public figures.

A Generational Relationship

According to the International Society of Genetic Genealogy, a generation is a span of approximately twenty-five years. Oswald was born in 1939, Ray in 1928, and Sirhan in 1944. Their births covered a span of sixteen years, therefore it can be considered that all three men were products of the same generation.

Even though they were sixteen years apart, they were no doubt exposed to a similar overall societal experience from childhood.

Paternal Influence

The prestigious magazine *Psychology Today* gives a clear picture of the role of a father in a young man's life: "Even from birth, children who have an involved father are more likely to be emotionally secure, be confident to explore their surroundings, and, as they grow older, have better social connections. The way fathers play with their children also has an important impact on a child's emotional and social development."

Unfortunately, none of the three accused had a stable relationship with his father. Oswald's dad died of a heart attack two months before his birth, so he was raised without a father.

When Ray was seven years old, his dad had a run-in with the law and moved the family from Illinois to Missouri to escape prosecution, and he even changed the family's surname to hide from police.

Sirhan's father, while an active member of the family, was both strict and harsh and reportedly beat his children on a regular basis.

Clearly, none of the three had the emotional security and confidence that would normally be found in a loving family household.

Religious Upbringing

Both Oswald and Ray were raised in the Catholic faith, although neither was still practicing in their adulthood.

Sirhan, on the other hand, changed religions a number of times, from Baptist to Seventh Day Adventist, then to an occult religion called the "Ancient and Mystical Order Rosæ Crucis."

Psychology Today published an article in 2014 concerning the ties between religious upbringing and personal stability. It noted, "As one finds relationships through a congregation, one also experiences a sense of belonging and even an identity associated with inclusion. One might feel older through a rite of passage like a bar mitzvah, and the routine and predictability of daily prayer can give a child the sense that at least one part of his world is predictable."

In other words, a religious upbringing anchors a child in his youth, and gives him a sense of stability and being included in a greater purpose.

None of the three accused, neither Oswald, Sirhan, nor Ray, had the benefits of a consistent religious upbringing. The early exposure that diminished as they grew could have left them feeling alone, dejected, and wanting for something more.

Geographic Location

Instead of having stable, permanent home environments, all three men were moved around in the course of their youth.

Oswald was born in New Orleans, moved to Dallas, then to New York, and finally back to New Orleans again.

169

Ray was born in Illinois, and at the age of seven, his family moved to Bowling Green, Missouri, to escape the police, and finally to Ewing, Missouri.

Sirhan was born in Jerusalem, then his family moved to New York when he was twelve, and then on to California.

A study published in the *Journal of Social and Personality Psychology* reports that family moves are tough on kids and usually disrupt important friendships. These effects are most problematic for kids who are introverted and those whose personalities tend toward anxiety and inflexibility. Moves are also hardest on children in the midst of other transitions – such as puberty and school changes. Middle school seems to be the toughest time to make a transition.

Education

All three of the accused men bounced around the educational system at different levels.

Oswald attended several different schools in his youth, finally dropping out of high school at the age of seventeen.

Ray moved schools from Illinois to Missouri, and he finally dropped out of high school at the age of fifteen.

While Sirhan completed high school, he couldn't find his way in a college career, and so he simply dropped out.

National Public Radio recently reported that "the unemployment rate for people without a high school diploma is nearly twice that of the general population. Dropouts are more likely to commit crimes, abuse drugs and alcohol, become teenage parents, live in poverty and commit suicide." Clearly this is not a good picture for those dropping out of an education program, like the three accused.

Military Service

When Oswald quit high school in the tenth grade, he went into the Marine Corps and was stationed in Japan. He showed an interest, if not an obsession, with Marxism, and his fellow marines gave him the nickname "Osvaldovich."

Oswald in the Marines

Ray joined the Army when he dropped out of high school, but he had problems with his conduct while he was serving, resulting in a court-martial.

Of the three accused, only Sirhan never served in the military.

While military service has been a stabilizing factor to many, many people, it seemed to be an irritant for both Oswald and Ray. James Earl Ray was court-martialed for drunkenness and then given a general discharge for being inept, while Oswald was simply given an "undesirable discharge."

Careers

The header for this section is perhaps a misnomer because none of the three men ever held a steady job or worked toward a career with any longevity.

Oswald had a number of jobs; some of the highlights are his employment as a messenger boy, an office boy, and at a dental laboratory. He was also in the Marines, worked at a welding company, and finally had a job as an order filler at the Texas Schoolbook Depository.

Texas Schoolbook Depository

Ray started out his working life as an errand boy for the mistress of a brothel, and from there he moved into criminal activity, stealing and re-selling newspapers. He worked briefly at a shoe company before being dismissed, and then joined the Army. Afterward, he worked at a rubber company before serving time for burglary and armed robbery, and finally served a federal sentence for robbing a post office.

Sirhan worked in the stables of a racetrack, as a clerk in a health food store, and had an erratic history of employment in his life.

Again, none of the three ever had a career plan or even a cohesive work history. They bounced from job to job before ending up in the situations that ended up defining their lives.

Final Thoughts on the Accused...

I am not a psychotherapist, psychologist, or criminal analyst by any stretch of the imagination, and it isn't my intention to pass myself off as such. I just like to think of myself as a rancher and a country lawyer.

But having said that, it should be clear to the most casual observer that the three accused assassins, Lee Harvey Oswald, Sirhan Sirhan, and James Earl Ray, were all strikingly similar in the areas that were outlined in this chapter. They all walked very similar paths from their birth to the time when they were accused of killing three of the most important men of the 20th Century.

- They all had family issues, specifically with their fathers.
- None of them had a stable religious upbringing.
- All moved around a number of times during their youths, taking away the stability of friends and routine.
- The three had issues in the educational system.
- Two of the three had issues in the military.
- None had career aspirations or held any long-time job.

Conspiracy theorists would call these into evidence that they were the perfect candidates to be recruited as patsies for the murders that they were accused of committing. On the other hand, perhaps these were just the kind of blind followers that Mr. Hunt was trying to reach with his *Life Line* program.

Perhaps they had other external influences in their lives that might have led them to participate in, and be accused of, each of the heinous murders... murders that they would all three denounce.

173

Part VIII: Epilogue

Haroldson Lafayette Hunt died on November 29, 1974, at Dallas' Baylor University Medical Center. His assassin was pneumonia, along with complications from cancer. The open-casket funeral was held at the First Baptist Church of Dallas and was officiated by none other than the Rev. W.A. Criswell himself.

Mr. Hunt and I had parted ways five years earlier, when I resigned from the company on November 14, 1969. Some of the Hunt children were getting involved in their dad's business and accusations and allegations were flying every direction. You can read all the stories on the Internet and in books, magazines, and newspapers. There may be some truth to some of the tales, but there's certainly a lot of hogwash that gets thrown around in them as well.

Looking back, I had a lot of interesting experiences during the time that I was associated with Mr. Hunt. I went to fascinating places, met powerful people, and did things that I would otherwise never have. For example, I can't tell you how many times I've boarded an airplane with a briefcase full of money to deliver across the country... not a lot of people can say that. And in today's world, it would be impossible to do.

As I look around me, I find that most everyone else involved from this time is gone – I'm the sole survivor, the last man standing, and I simply want to tell my story. Like I've said all along, it's not my intention to make anyone believe anything… I'm simply telling you the true stories about what happened with Mr. Hunt and his motive and opportunity concerning these four men.

I was party to most of Mr. Hunt's business, with the exception of those curious instances that I've described in this book… his meeting with Marina Oswald, the money that went to L.A. after Robert Kennedy's killing, and some of the other things that I've mentioned.

I have always assumed that things with these four murders happened just the way that the officials said: that Lee Harvey Oswald acted alone in shooting President Kennedy, that James Earl Ray shot Martin Luther King outside of that Memphis hotel room, that Sirhan Sirhan gunned down Bobby Kennedy in Los Angeles, and that Jimmy Hoffa's death was simply another mob execution.

Sometimes, though, I have to stop and think about the strange experiences that I had with Mr. Hunt concerning those four people and their deaths. I remember Oswald calling out, "I'm a patsy," James Earl Ray denying any involvement in King's shooting (and King's family believing him), and Sirhan Sirhan having absolutely no recollection of shooting Bobby Kennedy. To add to that, Bobby Kennedy is calling for a re-opening of the investigation into his father's death. After visiting Sirhan Sirhan in prison, he simply does not believe that the convicted man fired the fatal shot. Of course, no one has been identified as Hoffa's killer… and probably never will, although there has been a lot of speculation.

There's one more thing that I should mention – I've been hesitant to do so, because quite honestly, even though it's the absolute truth, it sounds a little far out. My original intent was to leave it out of the book, but as I'm wrapping things up, I believe that it deserves to be written down.

During the period of time before the 1960 Democratic Convention and continuing after that, H.L. Hunt became more and more interested in what he called a "Removal Group." That sounded all nice, clean and sterile, but it was far from that. I nicknamed it the "Kill Squad," because that is what it was really going to be. Mr. Hunt always believed that his programs *Facts Forum* and *Life Line* would, over time, convince a certain type of listener to do things in accordance with the dogma that these programs were putting forward.

In some of the more serious situations, however, it was clear that *Life Line* might simply be too slow. If Mr. Hunt could develop a "Removal Squad," then in that event, results could take place almost overnight.

Remember that Joe Civello, the Dallas organized crime boss, had given Mr. Hunt some information that I have previously mentioned in the book: It would definitely be possible to kill an important public figure and to keep the assassin from revealing the plan, you would simply kill the killer. If that were impossible, it would be necessary to make sure that the assassin pleaded guilty to the murder himself, which would stop any further investigation.

Based on Civello's information, a unique plan was developed and organized. Mr. Hunt wanted to establish four separate groups, each operating independently of each other, totally compartmentalized, and with no contact among the groups.

1) The job of the first group would be to determine who might be a candidate for "removal." They would

make suggestions based on the individual's political beliefs, their ability to get results that had opposite purposes of H.L. Hunt, and their ability to have an influence on other people.

2) The second group would then take those names and develop a detailed history of their lifestyle, including where they lived, where they worked, where their family was located and their everyday habits – both good and bad.

3) The third group would develop a plan of how that person could be most easily "removed." Mr. Hunt did not want just a shooting death; that would be too messy and draw way too much attention. Instead, the preferred death for the mark would involve an accident, drug overdose, family matter, or even an unexplained case. That was Mr. Hunt's goal.

4) The fourth group, based upon all the independent information provided by the other groups, would evaluate the situation and the person, make the final decision as to how it would be carried out, and then arrange for the final event. Afterwards, the affair could be cleaned up in the manner described by Joe Civello.

What Mr. Hunt hoped to accomplish was to have as much insulation as possible surrounding the removal of a particular person – to have the "Removal Squad" groups act independently of each other. This would give a high degree of insulation and protection between the group that said, "This person should be removed," and the group that said, "Let's do it."

To my knowledge, this entire "Removal Squad" plan – or "Kill Squad" as I called it – never moved past the planning phase. The first three potential targets were identified, however. The first was a U.S. Senator from California, the second was a Congressman from New York, and the third was a powerful leader from Santa Domingo. I still remember their names, but it wouldn't serve any purpose to call them out here.

I do have to say, however, that in looking back at history, when JFK was killed, his assassin Lee Harvey Oswald was shot in very short order... the "killer was killed," as Mr. Civello advised.

When James Earl Ray pled guilty, I remembered Mr. Civello's third rule, and it seemed to play directly into that.

Coincidence? Possibly. Still, it appears that – at least on the surface – there could have been other elements at work in these killings, and some of them could have been provided by my former employer, H.L. Hunt.

After all, he had both the motive and opportunity.

Yours respectfully,
John Curington

Afterword by Mitchel Whitington

At my first meeting with John Curington, we were in the initial few minutes of our conversation and he said, "You don't know anything about me, and I don't know anything about you, so that puts us on a level playing field."

John went on to state that he had wanted to work with a writer that did not have any preconceived ideas or theories involving the subject that he wanted to write about – the four men who met untimely deaths: John F. Kennedy, Martin Luther King, Bobby Kennedy, and Jimmy Hoffa.

John wanted to focus on one person, H.L. Hunt, who it seemed, in fact, did have the motive and opportunity to be involved in the deaths of all four of these men – all easily recognizable and influential national figures.

For the next several months we talked quite often and tried to meet every few days at a place called *David Beard's Catfish Village*, a restaurant in Ore City, Texas. With the delicious food and delightful staff, for us, it served as the perfect office for our discussions.

Toward the end of these meetings when the book was almost finished, John confessed that in fact, he did know a few things about me. As it turned out, he'd had me checked out very thoroughly and it surprised me how much he knew about me. That's okay, though, because I was flattered by the kind things that he said.

At our "desk" – John Curington and Mitchel Whitington

At one point, John asked me whether I believed there was a conspiracy involving the death of those four men. We had been working on the *H.L. Hunt: Motive and Opportunity* book for some time, but his question caught me by surprise. My reply was, "Let me think about that." I did have a reply, but I wanted to organize my thoughts before giving him an answer.

Next time we met to work on the book, I told him four things:

1) After writing his story, I do believe that there was a conspiracy; however, like any good conspiracy, it was both invisible and intangible.

2) H.L. Hunt's *Life Line* radio program had an estimated five million listeners, and he had used it in a masterful way against these men long before they were killed.

3) I think it's a fact that *Life Line* was produced and distributed solely to express the views of H.L. Hunt concerning who was good or bad on a national level, and particularly to single out those who Hunt felt needed to be ousted from public life.

4) The killers of three of the men, Oswald, Ray, and Sirhan, all had very similar backgrounds. Their childhood experience, educational history, employment record, and low self-esteem gave them the potential to become cold-blooded assassins. But did each of them actually pull the trigger to launch the killing bullet? After spending so much time in John's world, I have my doubts. To what extent was Mr. Hunt involved? Well, I'll leave such speculations up to you, the reader.

Coincidentally, as we finished this book, new records about the Kennedy assassination were being released by the National Archives in accordance with the JFK Assassination Records Collection Act. Once again, Kennedy's killing was making headlines.

Another headline came out that Robert Kennedy's son was looking into his murder, and not only had examined the police findings and autopsy files, but had also visited Sirhan Sirhan in prison. Kennedy stated for the record that he did not believe that Sirhan was the person who had killed his father. At the time of this writing, he has been calling for a re-opening of the case.

As I worked with John, I paid much closer attention to the news as it came out, with a heightened sense of interest. When Dr. Wecht gave us a Foreword for this book, I also began to study his incredible observations on not only JFK, but Martin Luther King and RFK as well.

That, along with the many items that I've been able to verify with research, has convinced me that John's accounts given in this book are not only completely honest and accurate, but also provide an insight into the assassination of four of the most powerful men in the county during the 1960s and 70s.

I believe that Haroldson Lafayette Hunt was involved in the deaths of these men, at least to the extent proposed by John Curington and probably beyond.

To reiterate the words John used earlier, Mr. Hunt had both the motive and opportunity... but perhaps he had even more.

Best regards,
Mitchel Whitington

Illustration Notes

Introduction by Author Mitchel Whitington

Mitchel Whitington – photo courtesy of the author.

Introduction by Dr. Cyril Wecht, M.D, J.D.

Dr. Cyril Wecht – photo courtesy of Dr. Wecht.

Part I: My Name is John Curington

World's Fair photograph by Ron White. This work has been released into the public domain by its creator.

Wild Mouse Roller Coaster photograph by Deron Meranda. This work has been released into the public domain by its creator.

Robert Moses – from the Library of Congress. This work is from the New York World-Telegram and Sun collection at the Library of Congress. According to the library, there are no known copyright restrictions on the use of this work. This photograph is a work for hire created prior to 1968 by a staff photographer at New York *World-Telegram and Sun*. It is part of a collection donated to the Library of Congress and per the instrument of gift it is in the public domain.

Lyndon Johnson – This United States Congress image is in the public domain. This may be because it was taken by an employee of the Congress as part of that person's official duties, or because it has been released into the public domain and posted on the official websites of a member of Congress. As a work of the U.S. federal government, the image is in the public domain.

John Curington photograph by Dixon Cartwright on 7/28/2017. Used with permission.

Farmersville, Texas – photograph taken in 1900. This image is in the public domain; this applies to U.S. works where the copyright has expired because its first publication occurred prior to January 1, 1923.

Dallas Texans Logo – from a promotional sticker in the collection of the author.

H.L. Hunt Letter – from the files of John Curington.

H.L. Hunt Letter – from the files of John Curington.

H.L. Hunt Letter – from the files of John Curington.

Part II: H.L. Hunt

H.L. Hunt photograph – this advertisement (or image from an advertisement) is in the public domain because it was published in a collective work (such as a periodical issue) in the United States between 1923 and 1977 and without a copyright notice specific to the advertisement.

H.L. Hunt in 1911 – this image is in the public domain; this applies to U.S. works where the copyright has expired because its first publication occurred prior to January 1, 1923.

East Texas Oil Field in 1919 – this image is in the public domain; this applies to U.S. works where the copyright has expired because its first publication occurred prior to January 1, 1923.

Taxi Cab – this image is a work of an Environmental Protection Agency employee, taken or made as part of that person's official duties. As works of the U.S. federal government, all EPA images are in the public domain.
Knife and pecans – photo by Mitchel Whitington.

Copy of KERA Press Release – from the files of John Curington.

Gun – photo by John Curington.

Stardust Hotel and Casino – photograph by Simon Johansson. This work has been released into the public domain by its creator.

Adlai Stevenson from the Library of Congress. This work is from the New York World-Telegram and Sun collection at the Library of Congress. According to the library, there are no known copyright restrictions on the use of this work. This photograph is a work for hire created prior to 1968 by a staff photographer at New York *World-Telegram and Sun*. It is part of a collection donated to the Library of Congress and per the instrument of gift it is in the public domain.

Discovery Well Photo – this image is in the public domain because it was published in a collective work (such as a periodical issue) in the United States between 1923 and 1977 and without a copyright notice specific to the advertisement.

H.L. Hunt Letter – from the files of John Curington.

Mount Vernon – Library of Congress, Prints & Photographs Division, photograph by Carol M. Highsmith. Highsmith, a distinguished and richly-published American photographer, has donated her work to the Library of Congress since 1992. Starting in 2002, Highsmith provided scans or photographs she shot digitally with new donations to allow rapid online access throughout the world. Her generosity in dedicating the rights to the American people for copyright free access also makes this Archive a very special visual resource. Publication and other forms of distribution: Ms. Highsmith has stipulated that her photographs are in the public domain.

Part III: Mr. Hunt and JFK

John F. Kennedy – this image is a work of an employee of the Executive Office of the president of the United States, taken or made as part of that person's official duties. As a work of the U.S. federal government, the image is in the public domain.

The 1960 Democratic National Convention – This work is in the public domain in the United States because it is a work prepared by an officer or employee of the United States Government as part of that person's official duties under the terms of Title 17, Chapter 1, Section 105 of the US Code.

Lyndon Baines Johnson – This image is a work of an employee of the Executive Office of the president of the United States, taken or made as part of that person's official duties. As a work of the U.S. federal government, the image is in the public domain.

RFK and LBJ – This work is in the public domain in the United States because it is a work prepared by an officer or employee of the United States Government as part of that person's official duties under the terms of Title 17, Chapter 1, Section 105 of the US Code.

General Edwin Walker – This work is in the public domain in the United States because it is a work prepared by an officer or employee of the United States Government as part of that person's official duties under the terms of Title 17, Chapter 1, Section 105 of the US Code.

Kennedy Motorcade by Walt Cisco, *The Dallas Morning News*. This work is in the public domain; copyright expired in 1991 without renewal. First published on November 24, 1963.

Ruby Shooting Oswald – This work is in the public domain; copyright expired because the work was published without a copyright notice and/or without the necessary copyright registration.

Civello Obituary – copyright by and courtesy of the Dallas Times Herald.

Dear Mr. Hunt Letter – copy from the files of John Curington. The original was given to the FBI.

Marina Oswald – Warren Comm. Files Exhibit No. 2595. This work is in the public domain in the United States because it was published in the United States between 1923 and 1977 without a copyright notice.

Hubert H. Humphrey – This work is in the public domain in the United States because it is a work prepared by an officer or employee of the United States Government as part of that person's official duties under the terms of Title 17, Chapter 1, Section 105 of the US Code.

Part IV: Mr. Hunt and Martin Luther King

Martin Luther King – This Swedish photograph is in the public domain because one of the following applies: The work is non-artistic (journalistic) and has been created before 1969. The photographer is not known, and cannot be traced, and the work has been created before 1944.

Rosa Parks being fingerprinted after her arrest – This work is in the public domain in the United States because it was published in the United States between 1923 and 1977 without a copyright notice.

The Assassination Scene, Lorraine Motel, Memphis – Library of Congress, Prints & Photographs Division, photograph by Carol M. Highsmith. Highsmith, a distinguished and richly-published American photographer, has donated her work to the Library of Congress since 1992. Starting in 2002, Highsmith provided scans or photographs she shot digitally with new donations to allow rapid online access throughout the world. Her generosity in dedicating the rights to the American people for copyright free access also makes this Archive a very special visual resource. Publication and other forms of distribution: Ms. Highsmith has stipulated that her photographs are in the public domain.

Part V: Mr. Hunt and Bobby Kennedy

Bobby Kennedy – This work is from the New York World-Telegram and Sun collection at the Library of Congress. According to the library, there are no known copyright restrictions on the use of this work. This photograph is a work for hire created prior to 1968 by a staff photographer at New York *World-Telegram and Sun*. It is part of a collection donated to the Library of Congress and per the instrument of gift it is in the public domain.

The Ambassador Hotel – This work has been released into the public domain by its author, English Wikipedia at English Wikipedia. This applies worldwide.

Sirhan Sirhan – This work was created by a government unit (including state, county, and municipal government agencies) of the State of California and is subject to disclosure under the Public Records Act. It is a public record that was not created by an agency which state law has allowed to claim copyright and is therefore in the public domain in the United States.

Report – from the files of John Curington.

Part VI: Mr. Hunt and Jimmy Hoffa

Jimmy Hoffa – This work is from the New York World-Telegram and Sun collection at the Library of Congress. According to the library, there are no known copyright restrictions on the use of this work. This photograph is a work for hire created prior to 1968 by a staff photographer at New York *World-Telegram and Sun*. It is part of a collection donated to the Library of Congress and per the instrument of gift it is in the public domain.

Postcard from the Cabana Motor Hotel – from the author's collection.

Part VII: The Accused

Lee Harvey Oswald – This work was created by a government unit (including state, county, and municipal government agencies) and is subject to disclosure under the Public Records

Act. It is a public record that was not created by an agency which state law has allowed to claim copyright and is therefore in the public domain in the United States.

James Earl Ray – This image is a work of a United States Department of Justice employee, taken or made as part of that person's official duties. As a work of the U.S. federal government, the image is in the public domain (17 U.S.C. § 101 and 105).

Sirhan Sirhan – This work was created by a government unit (including state, county, and municipal government agencies) of the State of California and is subject to disclosure under the Public Records Act. It is a public record that was not created by an agency which state law has allowed to claim copyright and is therefore in the public domain in the United States.

Oswald in the Marines – This work is in the public domain in the United States because it is a work prepared by an officer or employee of the United States Government as part of that person's official duties under the terms of Title 17, Chapter 1, Section 105 of the US Code.

Texas Schoolbook Depository – This work is in the public domain in the United States because it is a work prepared by an officer or employee of the United States Government as part of that person's official duties under the terms of Title 17, Chapter 1, Section 105 of the US Code.

Index

Ed. Note: H.L. Hunt appears on most every page of the book, so it would be meaningless to include him in the index. The same is true with the four other subjects: John Kennedy, Martin Luther King, Bobby Kennedy and Jimmy Hoffa.

CPSIA information can be obtained
at www.ICGtesting.com
Printed in the USA
BVHW051358070821
613846BV00010B/1205